THE COUNTRY OF FIRST BOYS

AMARTYA SEN

THE COUNTRY
OF
FIRST BOYS

and other essays

edited by
Antara Dev Sen
Pratik Kanjilal

The Little Magazine

OXFORD
UNIVERSITY PRESS

OXFORD
UNIVERSITY PRESS

Oxford University Press is a department of the University of Oxford.
It furthers the University's objective of excellence in research, scholarship,
and education by publishing worldwide. Oxford is a registered trademark of
Oxford University Press in the UK and in certain other countries

Published in the
United States of America by
Oxford University Press
198 Madison Avenue, New York, NY 10016

© *The Little Magazine* 2015

The moral rights of the authors have been asserted

First Edition published by *The Little Magazine*, New Delhi,
and Oxford University Press India in 2015

ISBN-13:978-0-19-873818-3 (hardcover)

Printed in the United States of America

To schoolteachers and health workers

CONTENTS

FOREWORD

New years are marked by an abundance of calendars. They come in all shapes and forms. 'Wall-type' ones, after they have been extricated with sharp instruments from their cylindrical holds, remain slaves to their upbringing and are put up on a wall only to curl up again. 'Desk-type' ones, with their pretty pictures all but concealing the dates and days, perch most unsatisfactorily on the piece of furniture they are named after. Those that come in squat publications that are little more than advertisements wearing the garb of dates are a waste of space and of time, especially when they insist on telling me which hours of the day are auspicious, which are not, and which are positively disastrous for enterprises outside the routines of ablutions and digestion.

I keep only the calendars which tell the date and day of the week with bold-font clarity and with no agenda other than that of being a calendar. I give the rest away. Nonetheless, I am glad to get all the calendars that come my way.

Why?

Let Amartya Sen tell us.

Amartya Sen? Surely, he has more important things to write about!

More important? The Professor of Economics and Philosophy at Harvard has to have his own sense of what is important. Calendars are among them. I reproduce two sentences from his piece 'India Through Its Calendars' in this volume.

'The need for a calendar has been strongly felt—and well understood—well before the modern age.'

'Different ways of seeing India—from purely Hinduism-centred
views to intensely secular interpretations—are competing
with each other for attention.'

No one who reads those two lines can resist reading on and
learning from that essay the hows and whys and wherefores of
India's calendrical heritage as contained in the Kaliyuga calendar, the Buddha Nirvana calendar, the Mahavira Nirvana
one, and the ones known as Vikram Samvat, Saka, Vedanga
Jyotisha, Islamic Hijri, Parsee, the Bengali San, and the Kollam—down to the Christian date systems and the exercises of
Dr Meghnad Saha, 'the leader of calendar reform in India'.

Indeed, through that essay on calendars, we can access facets
of Indian cultural settings and situations, especially those
derived from its astronomical enquiries, over millennia. More
significantly, we can gain new empirical insights into our past
from Sen's discussion of the 'zero points' employed by different calendars as their scaling device. And what a curtain call
of Indian history that piece gives us! Sen tells us: "The often-
repeated belief that India was a 'Hindu country' before Islam
arrived is, of course, a pure illusion, and the calendrical story
fits well into what we know from other fields of Indian history."
That, one might say, is a sound fist raised by a secular hand. But
he comes straight into the pulsations of daily living when, after
telling us when and how and why the Bengali solar calendar
was 'adjusted' to the lunar Hijri number in the San, he says:
"When a Bengali Hindu does religious ceremonies according
to the local calendar, he or she may not be quite aware that the

dates ... are attuned to commemorating Mohammad's journey from Mecca to Medina ..."

I have read the pieces compiled in this volume as essays are meant to be read—without an appetite for knowledge, a thirst for data or hunger for measurable quantities of explanation. I have read them for and with the pleasure that comes, almost incidentally, with insights. Even delicious fare might bring with it nourishment.

I have heard it said in a few places, but nowhere more emphatically than in Kolkata, that Amartya Sen's place in the world of thought is assured by what he has written on welfare economics and on social choice. Technically minded commentators have gone into nuances and told me, almost as if letting me into a secret, as to how, in fact, the econometrician outweighs the economist in the great man's intellectual chemistry. I have not doubted, much less questioned, this. How can I? I know neither the big and the bold nor the nice and the nuanced about any of those subjects. And yet, something in me has resisted that categorization as being polemical. If there is such a being as the 'argumentative Indian', there is another equally authentic one in the hair-splitting Indian, or the one who to match the *abhiprayabhedi* might, in a Sanskrit neologism, be called the *kesachhedi*.

A classical singer can give us a full-bodied *alap* followed by the carefully calibrated rendition of his chosen *raga*, but that does not preclude his creating a *ragamalika* of fragments as well, borrowed from different *ragas* set to varied *talas* and strung together in a pleasant yet skilled miscellany of modes and moods. Essays by a practitioner of the 'paper' genre are exactly those, un-heavy without being light, informal without being casual, not 'out to prove' or to establish a theory or a line of thought but only to share perceptions.

This sharing of the 'side thought' is, with Amartya Sen, not unlike a bicycle track that runs beside the main road. But it does not thereby become any the less as a talent and a preoccupation. I say this with what may be called the internal evidence of his writing style. Examine Sen's most formal works, as different from his occasional pieces, and even there you will find him using that most endearing, thought-varying, monotony-breaking, conversational punctuation mark, the em dash (–), which marks a break of thought, a change of emphasis, or the interpolation of a related but separate idea, within the parent stream of thought. The two 'calendar' quotations I have given contain the em dash, typically. (The term 'em dash' derives from its defined width of one M, as distinct from the smaller 'en dash' which corresponds in width to one N, and of course, as distinct from the even smaller, 'half N' or hyphen.)

I think Sen's prodigious, almost compulsive, use of the em dash is in-deliberate. I would not be surprised if he were hearing this said of his punctuational method for the first time. And it is well that it is so, for in his un-rehearsed, almost unconscious use of this rare but punctuationally legitimate mode lies its effectiveness and its charm. It is that which makes it his style and his practice, rather than a gambit and a ploy.

A typical example: 'For example, many countries have experienced—and continue to experience—the simultaneous presence of economic destitution and political strife.'

A classical example: 'The central question is not—indeed cannot be—whether or not to use the market economy.'

A telling example: 'We have to appreciate the importance of the voice that play can give to people—even to the underdog—in their attempt to counter tyranny or exploitation or deep inequality.'

An instructive example: 'Nothing brings out the poverty of India today as much as the state of many—indeed most—of our children.'

A memorable inter-connected one (not in this volume) on the Indian news media and misreporting:

> ... yet the celebration of the Indian media can go only so far—and no further ... As an Indian reader I would like to be sure, when I open a newspaper, that what I am reading—that A said B—is actually accurate ... Dozens of pages of denunciation materialized ... The one I liked the best said: 'I think Mr. Sen should keep his mouth shut'—an eminently sensible piece of advice, given the constant danger of misreporting ...

Is there a significance to Sen's taking repeated and persistent recourse to the em dash? Without over-tuning the point, let me say I believe there is and explain it as follows.

The advancing of a proposition, a hypothesis, or a simple viewpoint can be done either magisterially or conversationally. If the former, oracular aphorisms would suffice; if the latter, the exercise would be akin to a negotiation, in which the proponent suggests something with the confidence of intellectual conviction but with the humility of a discussant as well, emphasizing, stressing, exemplifying, modifying, conjugating, divagating, fluxing, disaggregating and aggregating, and qualifying the thesis, or, in other words, making the point a coalition of thoughts rather than 'a given'. This would also involve anticipating counter-arguments, counter-proposals, exceptions, examples, and building them into the narrative. The proponent's own 'line' becomes, in the hands of the 'negotiating' writer, a vehicle of persuasion as much as of ratiocination.

In the fields of Amartya Sen's large and growing interests, for example, history, philosophy, sociology, political theory, and linguistics, generalizations are risky and admonitory or affirmative prescriptions fatal. There are far too many complexities to the themes in question, far too many caveats to be made and codicils to be spelt out, to permit an unpunctuated, un-variegated, un-nuanced syntax. Besides, his own sense of fairness requires him to 'em' his dashes and make his sentences marsupial. They carry within themselves young and independent examples that corroborate a point by entrenching it with an analogy, or carry exceptions that show the point's limitations.

This is also connected to Sen being what may be called an intellectual democrat, in that he seeks to assign to fragments of thoughts, disjointed or discontinuous as they may be, the same position within a sentence as the un-fragmented 'central point'. There lies the classiness of his thinking and its confidence. Far from weakening his proposition, such a terracing of the thought only makes it stronger and more resilient.

One master of this art—for it is no less than an art—was George Orwell. In his celebrated essay titled 'Benefit of Clergy', Orwell says of Salvador Dali that the master painter was at once "a good draughtsman and a disgusting human being". If an em dash was to have been employed by Orwell, he would have said "Dali, a good draughtsman—though a rotten human being—

etc., etc. ..." But Orwell was pronouncing judgement and, in my opinion, a very fair one; he was not trying to negotiate a change of widely held opinions.

Sen is trying to convince, not inform, his readers, whence his use of that supple mark.

The examples of Sen's writing incorporated in this nugget of a volume reflect the sweep of his speculations, their ability to absorb the penumbra, and the nimbus around the central core of his thoughts. To that extent, they typify the spirit of the *Prasnopanishad*, which answered the mind's enquiries as much through questions as through responses, and as much through the embracing of genuine ambiguity as through the repulsing of feeble doubt.

The deconstruction of dogma through the admittance of enquiry is a matter of style as much as it is of substance. It is an act of reason as much as it is an aesthetic performance, for symmetry belongs to Euclid alone, while we lie scattered in the calendars, almanacs, and 'zero points' of many and often contradictory affiliations and affinities.

To have had the chance of hearing and reading one who claims an earnest seeking of facts, not infallible certitudes, is to have heard a voice over noise.

In the essay titled 'The Play's the Thing', Sen says: "Voice is important, in demanding redress, in arguing forcefully, in insulting nicely, and for conversing, colluding, and contradicting. It is crucial, in general, for interacting, and this includes making good use of democracy." And he goes on to say, emming his dash: "And most importantly, voice through play—even a unilaterally devised play—can give the underdog an opportunity that he or she may not otherwise have."

The Little Magazine has given us Sen's voice at and through the 'play' that is as serious as his voice at 'work', for both give us an opportunity we cannot otherwise have of hearing that set of thoughts in so rare a timbre, pitch, and tone.

GOPALKRISHNA GANDHI

EDITORS' PREFACE

This book is like a time-lapse photograph shot over 15 years. These essays, presented in chronological order, under the broad heads of culture, society, and policy—most of which were first published in *The Little Magazine* (*TLM*) in the first decade of the twenty-first century—reflect concerns like terrorism and identity that dominated the politics of that time, in India and the world, and set the tone for the current era. They also contain insights that Amartya Sen would enlarge upon later, like the interesting dichotomy between the ideas of *niti* and *nyaya*. We have resisted the urge to make them 'contemporary'—an uncertain enterprise in a rapidly evolving world—because in interpreting the present, they already contained the germ of the future.

Some of these essays were specifically written for a particular *TLM* number. For instance, the essay 'Hunger: Old Torments and New Blunders' was written for our issue on hunger (where Sen actually took the time to read the essays that had reached us, in order to weave his comments on them into his own paper). Some are documents of record, like the print versions of the first Hiren Mukerjee Memorial Lecture, delivered in the Indian Parliament; and the Nadine Gordimer Lecture, delivered at Witwatsrand University and the University of Cape Town. Updating them would have amounted to doctoring the record. Some are documents of record of another kind. The essay on Nalanda University, for example, is like an elaborate birth certificate of the university. Through it, Sen maps

Nalanda in time and intellectual space, explains the idea of reviving the world's oldest university, and plants his hopes in this new garden of possibilities. The freshly reborn institution has just weathered its first struggle for academic independence. One day it will reach maturity, and it would be interesting to see how much of its parents' hopes and wishes it has fulfilled.

Of the 13 essays, two—'What Difference Can Tagore Make?' and 'A Wish a Day for a Week'—have not been published in *TLM*. They appear in print for the first time here, rounding off a series which shows that Amartya Sen's ideas from years ago remain drivers of the progressive quest for equality, justice, and empowerment even today. This does, sadly, reflect India's lack of significant progress in certain areas, like education and health care, which keep alive concerns that are decades old. But it also presents a moving picture of Indian society and culture, like a gallery of snapshots with timestamps. Very likely, the concerns and interests Sen has raised in these essays will remain of interest, with varying degrees of urgency, years in the future.

This volume—the first in the TLM–OUP series—would not have been possible without the unflagging enthusiasm and encouragement of Mini Krishnan, and the patience of the editorial team of OUP. We are grateful to A.S. Panneerselvan and Panos South Asia for their support in preparing the manuscript. Special thanks to Emma Rothschild for her incisive comments and advice. For all kinds of help in many different ways—from indexing and proofreading to printing out piles of text and other essentials—we thank Inga Huld Markan, Chie Ri, Namrata Narain, Anwesha Rana, and the ever-dependable Shailaja Gopalan. And, of course, this book owes most to Amartya Sen, most excellent of contributors who, despite a gruelling work schedule and an energetic public life, never missed *TLM*'s deadline in the 15 years that these essays span.

ANTARA DEV SEN
PRATIK KANJILAL
2015

INTRODUCTION

The Personal and the Social

The essays in this collection were written over a decade and a half, and they deal with a diversity of subjects.[1] If, nevertheless, there is something here that can be called a unity of approach, it must be connected with the fact that the articles all share an interest in India seen in a non-sectarian perspective, and reflect a concern with equity and justice, in different areas of human life—social, political, economic, cultural, and intellectual.

First a word on the title of this book—derived from the title of one of the essays included here. Major causes of injustice in India have historical as well as contemporary roots. When biases of one kind (for example, those based on caste or class) combine with other sources of disparity (such as gender), the oppression of the victim groups (such as girls from poor and low-caste families) can be massive and tyrannical. The 'country of first boys' can offer very different possibilities to boys from favoured backgrounds, which contrast sharply with the meagre opportunities that girls from underprivileged families get. The 'last girls' suffer not only from economic hardship, social deprivation, and political powerlessness, but also from a lack of opportunity to benefit from their intellectual potentials and from enjoying the rich intellectual heritage of India and the world.

[1] I am grateful to Pratik Kanjilal and Antara Dev Sen for selecting and editing these essays.

The articles included in this volume, which appear here roughly in the chronological order of their original publication (mostly in *The Little Magazine*), fall into three different categories, broadly related to culture, society, and policy. There are essays on Indian culture and the history of ideas (including the wealth of Indian calendars, the variety of Indian play and games, the story of the world's oldest university in Nalanda). There are analyses of hardened inequalities in Indian society, and the need to conquer the injustices they entail (related to class, caste, gender, community, and other barriers, yielding vastly diverse outcomes in nutrition, health, and education for different groups of Indians). And there are essays on policy issues, involving economic, political, and social reasoning.

I am fortunate that Gopal Gandhi—an old friend and an intellectual I greatly admire—has written a very kind and extremely enlightening Foreword to my attempted contributions in diverse subjects. Gopal Gandhi comments on the variety of my preoccupations that can be found here, reflecting—well, he is too kind and too good a friend to say it quite like that—my intellectual eccentricity. So, at the risk of being somewhat self-indulgent, I start there, and take the liberty of beginning with the warping of my mind—going back even to my school days.

Sanskrit and Mathematics

In my school days I was deeply involved with the study of Sanskrit, on one side, and with mathematical and analytical reasoning, on the other. Sanskrit captivated me, and I was very absorbed in the intricacies of the language and its enthralling literature. Indeed, for many years, Sanskrit was my second language, after Bengali. This was largely because my progress in English was very slow. Not being fluent in English was not a big inconvenience for me at that time, since I went to a Bengali-medium school (Patha Bhavan in Santiniketan).

In contrast with my neglect of English, there was no opportunity for me to lag behind in Sanskrit, since I had constant pressure at home to proceed further in Sanskrit, coming from my grandfather, Pundit Kshiti Mohan Sen (a great Sanskrit scholar). However, he did not have to push me very hard, since I was enchanted by the literature in Sanskrit (mostly classical Sanskrit, though I could also read, with a bit of help from my grandfather, some Vedic and epic Sanskrit, and also Pali). I became thoroughly engrossed also in the linguistic discipline of Sanskrit. Reading Panini was as exciting an adventure as any I have undertaken in my life—it taught me the basic demands of intellectual discipline.

There is a lot of advocacy these days on reviving the teaching of Sanskrit in Indian schools. I personally got so much from Sanskrit that I have to be basically sympathetic to that demand. More generally, I do believe that the case for studying a classical language in school is very strong—though that could also be Latin or Greek or Arabic or Hebrew or ancient Chinese or old Tamil. However, the advocacy of Sanskrit often comes from champions who see Sanskrit as the language of priesthood. That, of course, it also is, but Sanskrit has so much—indeed so *very* much—else. The epics are not primarily religious texts. Even the *Bhagavadgita* is only a small part of a grand epic, the Mahabharata, which presents visions that go well beyond the

Gita itself (what is described in the Mahabharata as the aftermath of the rightly won just war, with funeral pyres burning and women weeping about their lost men, is arguably closer to Arjuna's vision than to Krishna's). And the plays of Kalidasa, Shudraka, Bana, and others made me think about ideas and issues that greatly influenced my understanding of the world.

On the subject of religiosity, it is worth noting that Sanskrit—celebrated as a priestly language—also has a larger body of firmly agnostic and atheistic literature (in the works of Lokayata and of the Charvaka schools, among others), than any other classical language in the world.

And there is the reliably agnostic Gautama Buddha and his teachings. I have often wondered why I have been so deeply moved by Gautama Buddha, right from the time I first encountered his thoughts—when my grandfather gave me a short book on Gautama. I must have been about 11 or 12 then, and I remember that I was completely bowled over by the clarity of reasoning he used and the approachability he offered to all human beings—not just to Ananda, Subhuti, and his other disciples, but to anyone anywhere. Also, Buddha seemed to me to be clearly human, with our usual worries, in a way the powerful gods and goddesses were not. When young Gautama left his princely home in the foothills of the Himalayas in search of enlightenment, he was moved specifically by the sight of mortality, morbidity, and disability. What distressed him then, worries us even now.

As I was getting more and more inducted in the world opened up by Sanskrit, the analytical challenges of mathematics began capturing my mind as well. I remember my excitement when I first encountered the use of axioms, theorems, and proofs—how we can begin with one understanding and get many other understandings from it. I would have given everything to get a ticket to ancient Greece to go and invade the privacy of Euclid. The elegance and reach of interesting analytical proofs have engaged me throughout my life—and they still enthuse me. Indeed, I have spent a lot of my academic time in trying to establish results in social choice theory and decisional analysis for which my interest in the foundations of mathematical reasoning has been central.[2]

Luckily, I soon discovered that there was strong complementarity between my interest in Sanskrit and my involvement with mathematics. I greatly enjoyed the fact that I could easily move from Kalidasa's *Meghadootam* and Shudraka's *Mrichchhakatika* (among my favourite literary writings) to the mathematics and epistemology of Aryabhata, Brahmagupta, or Bhaskara (indeed both the Bhaskaras), without abandoning my love affair with Sanskrit.

Theories and Observations

If that duality—the diverse but ultimately compatible interest in Sanskrit and mathematics—was one diversity that shaped

[2] Happily for me, I get regular enjoyment every other year when I teach a course at Harvard on social choice theory jointly with Eric Maskin, an outstanding theorist—an enjoyment that was nicely supplemented recently by my teaching a course on 'reasoning by mathematical models' which Maskin and I co-taught with Barry Mazur (a great mathematician). The postgraduate course, full of talented and exciting students, was jointly offered by the mathematics and economics departments at Harvard.

my studies in school days, the fascination with abstract thinking, on the one hand, and my greedy curiosity about the world
around us, on the other, pulled me in somewhat different
directions. As I look back, at the age of 81, on the little work
I have been able to do in the course of my life, it seems to be
broadly divided into quite abstract reasoning (for example, in
pursuing the idea of justice and in exploring various avenues
in social choice theory, with axioms, theorems, and proofs) and
rather practical problems (famines, hunger, economic deprivations, inequalities of class, gender, and caste, and others).

I was forced to reflect on all that when the Nobel Foundation asked me to give them, on long-term loan, two objects that
have been closely associated with my work, for being displayed
in the Nobel Museum which would start in Stockholm and
tour the world. The generous citation with which the Swedish
Academy had announced my prize was heavily inclined in the
direction of my analytical work in social choice theory, quoting
chapters and verses (in fact, theorems and proofs), but they also
briefly mentioned, at the end of the statement, my work on
famines, inequality, and gender disparity. After some dithering
on which object to choose, I gave the Nobel Museum a copy of
Aryabhatiya (one of the great Sanskrit classics on mathematics
from AD 499) from which I had benefited so much, and my old
bicycle which had been with me from my school days.

I had used the bike not only to collect data on wages and
prices from fairly inaccessible places, like old farm sheds and
warehouses, for studying the Bengal famine of 1943, but also
for trips to Santiniketan's neighbouring villages to weigh boys
and girls up to the age of 5, to examine gender discrimina-
tion and the gradual emergence of the relative deprivation

of girls.[3] As the Nobel Museum, starting in Stockholm, went around the world, I often received questions about what a bike had to do with Aryabhata's mathematics. I had to explain why the answer had to be 'a great deal'.

Resisting Miniaturization of India

The India that emerged from my early studies had a greatness that I found hugely attractive. And to see, as my education continued, how that large tradition would be supplemented and further broadened by the reasoning and speculations of later thinkers (from Jayadeva and Madhavacharya to Kabir and Abul Faz'l) was altogether thrilling for me. If the greatness of the heritage captivated me, the attempts to redefine Indian culture in narrow, sectarian perspectives seemed to me to be immensely distressing. There was a lot of that going on when my school days were coming to an end and undivided India was becoming suddenly covered with competing versions of narrow-mindedness, along with accompanying intolerance, communal animosity, and bloodshed.

The understanding that human identity does not demand a singular confinement, came to me quite powerfully from the ancient classics. Think of Vasantasena, the heroine of

---

[3] I was tempted to give them the weighing machine we had used to measure the weights of young children to make cross-gender comparisons because I was disgracefully proud of the fact that I had to take over the task of weighing whenever my research assistant was deterred by bites from toothy children—I became the local expert on weighing without being bitten.

Shudraka's *Mrichchhakatika* from the fourth century. She is a great beauty, a rich courtesan, a dedicated lover and partner (of the persecuted Charudatta), a social reformer, a political revolutionary, and ultimately a forgiving judge, who supports her partner, Charudatta, in his decision to free the would-be murderer who had been trying to kill them both. As Charudatta's partner, she clearly applauds his farsighted decision to focus not on retribution, but on moral—and political—reform that would be in the best interest of the people. When Charudatta startles everyone (except possibly Vasantasena) with his judgement that it is the society's 'duty to "kill" the miscreant with benefaction' (the beautiful Sanskrit phrase for that innovative punishment—*upkarhatastakartavya*—fits as well on her lips as it does on his), something more than a new theory of jurisprudence is born. The same Vasantasena, who, earlier in the play, had spoken so eloquently and movingly on the injustice of inequality of power and of the corruption of the rich, joins Charudatta in rejecting revenge and pursuing a generosity that could have the effect of reforming the miscreants and helping that society to move on from its history of conflict and violence. Vasantasena—and Charudatta too—have many identities in Shudraka's revolutionary play focused on human well-being, from which there is so much to learn today—more than 1,500 years later.

There is an epistemic naivety in an attempt to identify a person exclusively by his or her membership of only one group—like Vasantasena being perceived only as a beautiful courtesan. In one of the essays, 'The Smallness Thrust upon Us' (which is based on a lecture I gave at the College de France), I have argued that this epistemic mistake can also lead to an ethical blunder, and possibly to a political disaster. Indeed, the propagation of a singular identity, based—respectively—on nationality, or religion, or race, or caste, has been responsible for a great deal of violence in different parts of the world, including massive bloodshed.

The importance of a clear-headed understanding of the stakes involved is no less at this time in India than it has ever been. We have reason to be proud of all significant achievements in India, whether they came from the Hindus, Muslims, Christians, Buddhists, Jains, Sikhs, Parsees, Jews, agnostics, or atheists. It is also important to appreciate that a culture—no matter what its religious accompaniments are (if any)—tends to involve many endeavours and pursuits other than religion. The richness of India's calendrical history, or the major contributions made in India in developing new and exciting games (of which the now-global game of chess is perhaps the best known), should be objects of attention and enquiry, even to understand the nature of India and its culture.

Let me illustrate. Reverence to the ancient Vedas is championed by many political advocates of religious persuasion in India today. I too share an exalted view of the Vedas. Not because I see it as the foundation of any religiosity I might have had. Nor because we can find any sophisticated mathematics there (despite the nicely engaging riddles that can be found in the *Atharva Veda*)—even though some universities in India have recently started giving postgraduate instructions on the allegedly academic subject of 'Vedic Mathematics'. India's giant contributions to the world of mathematics would come much later (led by Aryabhata, Brahmagupta, and others), and to look for them in the Vedas would be a big mistake.

What we have reason to cherish instead is the fact that the Vedas are full of wonderful verses—reflective, daring, elegant, and evocative. Many of the verses are beautifully religious, but they also include a powerfully articulated advocacy of agnosticism in the so-called 'Song of Creation' in the *Rig Veda*, mandala X, verse 129:

> Who knows, then whence it first came into being?
> He, the first origin of this creation,
> whether he formed it all or did not form it.
> Whose eye controls this world in highest heaven,
> he verily knows it, or perhaps he knows not.

When I first read the verse as a young boy, at a time when my own convictions as a disbeliever was taking root, I felt thrilled by the support coming from 3,500 years ago.

The intellectual history of India includes fun and scepticism—no less than religious thoughts of various kinds. Neither the majoritarian Hindu perspectives, nor any kind of multi-religious amalgam, can escape being a miniaturization of a great country.

Democracy and Social Commitment

I must move on from cultural matters to social, political, and economic issues. When India became independent, with democratic institutions of governance, the big famines that had characterized the long period of British rule in India came abruptly to an end. Famines were no longer feasible in a new, democratic India, with a free press, regular elections, and—most importantly—the involvement of the media in making the causation and preventability of famines widely known and understood.

How did this happen? The role of public reasoning in the achievements of democracy demands a clearer understanding. The proportion of the population affected or threatened by a famine is always small—hardly ever more than 10 per cent, and most often less than 5 per cent. So the question can be asked how a functioning majoritarian democracy can be so dedicated to, and so effective in, eliminating famines, which affects a small minority. The political compulsion in a democracy to eliminate famines depends critically on the power of public reasoning in making non-victims take on the need to eradicate famines as their *own* commitment. Democratic institutions can be effective only if different sections of the population appreciate what is happening to others, and if the political process reflects a broader social understanding of deprivation.

While democratic dialogue has taken on famine prevention as a social commitment, this has not yet happened with persistent hunger and chronic undernourishment, nor with continued illiteracy and massive lack of elementary health care. The ways and means of expanding the reach of public reasoning and social responsibility beyond the concerns of the relatively affluent are, thus, crucial for the future of India. It is, in fact, a central feature of democratic governance, which has to go well beyond merely holding regular elections.

The manifold deprivations of large sections of the Indian people can be removed only if serious political attention is paid to these disadvantages. It is certainly remarkable that India has more hungry people—including hungry children—than any other country in the world, but what is most

- persistent hunger
- chronic undernourishment
- continued illiteracy
- elementary health care

expanding the coverage and force of public reasoning

astonishing is how little attention this phenomenon has received, and how very reluctant the more prosperous—and more influential—parts of the population have been to allocate resources for the eradication of the disadvantages of the deprived.

The same applies to the continued absence of good elementary education and basic health care for large sections of the underprivileged in India. In a democracy these abysmal failures should receive massive political attention. The media has a huge role to play in this. If there is a tendency to neglect these major deprivations in the print and broadcast media, then Indian democracy, despite its strong institutional base, can be seen as failing to work properly. The prospects of a radical change in the prevalence of deep-rooted social injustice in India depend critically on the possibility of vastly expanding the coverage and force of public reasoning.

The Media and the Social Divide

Even though the media itself has a big responsibility for the bias in the coverage of news and analyses, the root of the problem of informational neglect lies in the hardened nature of the social divide in Indian society. There seems to be a serious lack of interest of the relatively privileged parts of society on matters of inequality and deprivation (despite the rhetoric often used in political campaigns), and the media tends to be shaped substantially by the need to cater to their regular subscribers as well as by support from advertisers. What is particularly striking about this media bias is the way the deep imbalance has managed to become almost invisible to the classes whose voices count and whose concerns dominate public discussion. A comparatively small group of the relatively privileged seems to have created a social universe of their own.[4]

The privileged group in India includes not only businessmen and the professional classes, but also the bulk of the country's relatively affluent, including the educated, classes. In a well-reasoned and powerful essay, called 'Emergence of the Intelligentsia as a Ruling Class in India',[5] Ashok Rudra argued several decades ago that the educated population of India, with a shared interest in the benefits to be derived from social inequality, has become part of the 'ruling coalition' which dominates policy discussions, and, as a consequence, also has an overpowering influence in what happens in the country. The 'relatively privileged' in this broad sense, perhaps a fourth or a fifth of the total population, comprise different strata—varying from tycoons, at one end, to educated ordinary people, at the other, who are not particularly rich, but enjoy levels of living that separate them from the masses of the underdogs of society.

It is the overarching division between the privileged and the rest that provides a backdrop to the contrast between the people whose lives get much attention in the media and public discussion, and the rest whose deprivations and despair are largely invisible in that communicational sphere. A huge

[4] On this see my joint book with Jean Drèze, *An Uncertain Glory: India and Its Contradictions* (Delhi and London: Penguin; and Princeton: Princeton University Press, 2013).

[5] Ashok Rudra, 'Emergence of the Intelligentsia as a Ruling Class in India', *Economic and Political Weekly*, volume 24, issue 3 (21 January 1989).

disparity between the privileged and the rest—notwithstanding their own internal divisions—fortifies the inequality of lives by an inequality of articulation and attention, which makes an overwhelming deprivation in the lives of people both less discussed and correspondingly more resilient and stable.

And yet things can change if we try. Neither the media, nor the intelligentsia, are really prisoners who cannot escape from their inherited role in the social division. Since the electoral victory of the Bharatiya Janata Party or BJP and its allies last year, the focus of public discussion has shifted somewhat towards the agenda of the Hindutva movement, but the social division in media coverage and the role of class-based divergence in informational bias continues in much the same way.

The Indian media not only tends to have a coverage bias, it often is also simply inaccurate. Bewildering misreporting is so common now that I have to confess that I am not surprised to read in the papers that I am a steadfast supporter of the Congress Party, or that I was an architect of the economic policies of the previous—United Progressive Alliance or UPA—government, policies that I had explicitly criticized in my writings.[6] In fact, many of the criticisms of the neglect of health and education under the previous government (and governments previous to that), and of the inaction in confronting deep-rooted inequality

[6] Gardiner Harris, reporting for *The New York Times*, asked me when writing on our book *An Uncertain Glory*, "Why do the newspapers say that you support the economic policies of the UPA, since you are constantly attacking them?" I don't think I managed to offer a satisfactory explanation to Harris, but I suppose it is presumed by some that if a person is critical of the BJP-led NDA, then he must be a supporter of the UPA and its economic programmes!

that I have been attacking for a long time (they figure prominently also in the joint book with Jean Drèze, *An Uncertain Glory:
India and Its Contradictions*), apply today under National Democratic Alliance or NDA government as well. To some extent the
rhetoric has changed, but a real change would require much
greater social radicalism in public reasoning than has been the
norm in India—today, yesterday, and the day before.

A change in this bias is, however, both possible and very
much needed, along with greater accuracy in news reporting.
In the political shift the contribution of the Indian left could
have been much greater than what their policy of muddling
through—and concentrating on peripheral issues rather than
the big social divide—has managed to yield (I have discussed
these issues in two essays in this collection, 'What Should Keep
Us Awake at Night' and 'A Wish a Day for a Week').

Economic Growth and Human Capability

Many of the mistaken reports are not particularly consequen-
tial. But I have to protest against one or two. The prevalence of
subsidies to those who are relatively better off—on electricity,
on diesel, on cooking gas, and others—is a consequence of the
same division of political power which I have been discussing,
and I have had the opportunity to criticize them consistently.
As I discuss in 'A Wish a Day for a Week', the amount spent
on subsidising the consumption of the relatively rich is many
times larger than what is spent on the much-attacked food subsidies and employment guarantees, taken together. If public
criticism coming from those with a strong voice is directed only

at the latter, and hardly at all against the former, then there is reason for us to take exception and to raise our voice, which I have tried to do. This does not make me 'pro-subsidy'—nor does it wash away the fact that I have consistently argued that subsidies to the better off should be altogether scrapped and even the food subsidies and employment guarantees need to be managed much better (in fact better organization and elimination of corruption are in the interest of the poor themselves).

The silence of many commentators on the subsidies for the benefit of those who are already well off, while thundering about the mismanagement of food and employment subsidies for the poor, reflects a class bias that we have every reason to confront. This bias is so strong in India that when the unexpected power failure suddenly happened in July 2012, the newspapers reported that 600 million Indians had been 'plunged into darkness', overlooking the fact that 200 million of those 600 million never had any electricity connection anyway and could not have been plunged into any *new* darkness.

To argue for the need to spend public funds to provide good state schools, functioning public health care, connections to power, and safe water for all can hardly be seen as advocacy of a 'subsidy' economy, unless we want to count countries like Japan, China, and South Korea to Britain, France, and Germany as 'subsidy' empires. The National Health Service with free medical care for all residents of Britain is not comparable to providing subsidies to the relatively affluent Indians for the use of cooking gas and underpriced electricity for those privileged enough to have equipment to use them.

The second issue concerns the mutually supporting relation between economic growth and the enhancement of human

[handwritten margin note top: crecimiento económico + mejoramiento de capacidades humanas]

capability, which I have tried to emphasize, arguing for both. I am, thus, mystified when I read, as I often do, that I am 'against' economic growth, and that I would want 'redistribution' instead. I should not have to go back to my PhD thesis (published as a book, *Choice of Techniques*, 1960), to note the fact that my main contribution in that work, if any, was to discuss the need to generate higher economic growth in choosing between technologies. Nor should I have to refer to the contents of my second book, *Growth Economics* (1970), inspired by the importance of economic growth. The central issue is not redistribution of income, but the provision of adequate and efficient public services (going beyond law and order), particularly related to education, health care, nutritional support, and environmental protection.

Aside from the misrepresentation of my beliefs and arguments, there is also a confusion in this critique in failing to see the complementarity between growth and capability formation.

While growth is important as an instrument for the advancement of people's well-being and freedom, growth-mania is not particularly useful, when it takes the form of regarding economic growth to be important in itself, rather than seeing it in terms of the opportunity it provides for enhancing people's lives. Growth has to be judged also in terms of how the fruits of economic growth are used. In the periods of high growth in India, both under UPA and NDA, the proportion of the proceeds of growth that went into enhancing the lives of people was low—indeed much lower than many countries, such as China and Indonesia, with which we want to compete in terms of the speed of economic growth.

*[handwritten margin note right: * Benefit sharing matters]*

However, the main problem in seeing economic growth as a conflicting priority with advancing health care and school

[handwritten note bottom: Benefit sharing = / provision of adequate and efficient public services (on environment protection)]

education in India (as some economists have tended to see it) lies in the fact that having an educated and healthy population can be a major contributor to enhancing steady and sustainable economic growth. It is the complementarity between education and health care, on one side, and economic growth, on the other, that laid the foundation of the rapid development of East Asia—from Japan and South Korea to Taiwan, Singapore, Thailand, and China. India has missed out on making use of that basic wisdom. To want that mistake in understanding the causation of economic growth to be corrected is surely the very opposite of being 'anti-growth'.

There is plenty of empirical evidence from cross-country comparisons that brings out the basic fact that having an uneducated and unhealthy working population is not only bad for human well-being, it is also detrimental to steady and sustained economic growth.

The question can, however, be asked: how does universal health care become affordable in poor countries? The first—and perhaps the most important—factor overlooked by the naysayers is the fact that, at a basic level, health care is a very labour-intensive activity, and in a poor country wages are low. A poor country may be able to spend less money on health care, but it also needs to spend less to provide the same labour-intensive services (far less than what a richer—and high-wage—economy would have to pay). Not to take into account the implications of large wage differences is a gross oversight that distorts the discussion of the affordability of labour-intensive activities such as health care and education in low-wage economies.

Second, how much health care can be provided to all may well depend on the country's economic means. However, whatever is

* Collective good → unefficiently allocated by the pure market system.

affordable within a country's means can still be more effectively and more equitably provided through universal coverage.

Third, many medical and health services are shared, rather than being exclusively used by each individual separately. For example, an epidemiological intervention reaches many people who live in the same neighbourhood, rather than only one person at a time. Health care, thus, has strong components of what in economics is called a 'collective good', which can tend to be very inefficiently allocated by the pure market system, as has been extensively discussed by a number of economists, most notably by Paul Samuelson. Covering more people together can sometimes cost less than covering a smaller number individually.

Fourth, many diseases are infectious. Universal coverage prevents their spread and cuts costs through better epidemiological care. This point, as applied to individual regions, has been recognized for a very long time. The conquest of epidemics has, in fact, been achieved by not leaving anyone untreated in regions where the spread of infection is being tackled. The transmission of disease from region to region—and, of course, from country to country—has broadened the force of this argument in recent years.

Asymmetric Information and Health Care

In the absence of a reasonably well-organized system of public health care for all, many people are afflicted by overpriced and inefficient private health care, which is widespread in India. As has been analysed by many economists, most notably Kenneth Arrow, there cannot be a well-informed competitive market equilibrium in the field of medical attention because of what economists call 'asymmetric information'. This applies to the market for health insurance as well, since the insurance companies cannot fully know what the patients' health conditions are. This makes markets for private health insurance inescapably inefficient even in terms of the narrow logic of market allocation. And there is, in addition, the much bigger problem that private insurance companies, if unrestrained by regulations and scrutiny, have a strong financial interest in excluding patients who are taken to be 'high risk', and this defeats the purpose of universal health care. So one way or another, the government has to play an active part in making universal health care possible.

The problem of asymmetric information applies to the delivery of medical services itself. Patients do not typically know what treatment they need for their ailments, or what medicine would work, or even what exactly the doctor is giving to them as remedy. Unlike in the market for many commodities, such as shirts or umbrellas, the buyer of medical treatment knows far less than what the seller—the doctor—does, and this vitiates the efficiency of market competition. It makes the possibility of exploitation of the relatively ignorant a likely result even when there is plentiful market competition. And when medical personnel are scarce, so that there is not much competition either, it can make the predicament of the buyer of medical treatment even worse. Furthermore, when the providers of health care are not themselves trained (as is often the case in many parts of India), the situation becomes worse still. As a result, in the absence of a well-organized public health system covering all, many patients, denied of any alternative, remain vulnerable to exploitation by quacks, who can robustly combine crookery with their quackery.

In India, we see both systems operating side by side in different states within the country. Reliance on private practice for basic health is very often hugely exploitative, whereas public health care is frequently debilitated by the lack of work discipline and absenteeism and corruption of medical personnel.[7] And yet when the state-run medical services are run properly, they can provide a level of care to all that private medical delivery cannot, particularly because of the distortions from asymmetric information. A state like Kerala may provide fairly reliable basic health care for all through public services—Kerala pioneered universal health care in India several decades ago, through extensive public health services. As the population of Kerala has grown richer—partly as a result of universal health care and near-universal literacy—many people now choose to pay more and have more munificent private health care. But since these private services have to compete with what the state provides, and have to do even better to justify their charges in a region with widespread medical knowledge and medical opportunity with a stronger educational base, the quality of private medical services too tends to be bettered there than where there is a low level of public education and no competition from public medical services. In contrast, states like Madhya Pradesh or Uttar Pradesh give plentiful examples of exploitative and inefficient health care for the bulk of the population. Not surprisingly, people of Kerala live much longer and have a much lower incidence of preventable illnesses than do the population of states like Madhya Pradesh or Uttar Pradesh.

[7] On this see Drèze and Sen, 'India's Health Care Crisis', An Uncertain Glory, chapter 6. On the need for an interdisciplinary approach to understanding poverty, see also Deepa Narayan, Measuring Empowerment: Crossdisciplinary Perspectives (Washington, DC: World Bank, 2005).

A system of universal health care also has the advantage that it can focus on vitally needed—but often ignored—primary medical attention, and on relatively inexpensive outpatient care when a disease receives early attention. In the absence of systematic care for all, diseases are often allowed to grow, which makes it much more expensive to treat them, often involving inpatient treatment, such as surgery. Thailand's experience in recently introduced universal health care brings out sharply how the need for more expensive procedures tend to go down sharply with fuller coverage of preventive care and early intervention. Good health care demands systematic—and comprehensive—attention, and in the absence of affordable health care for all, illnesses become much harder—and also greatly more expensive—to treat. If the advancement of equity is one of the rewards of well-organized universal health care, enhancement of efficiency in medical attention is surely another.

A Test over Time

The complementary and mutually supportive relations between economic growth and the advancement of education and health is illustrated in the comparative experiences of different states within India. I remember being sternly admonished nearly 50 years ago, when I spoke in support of Kerala's efforts to have universal literacy and state-supported health care for all. I was firmly told that this strategy could not possibly work, since Kerala was then one of the poorest states in India. The thesis of unaffordability was, however, wrongly argued (for reasons already discussed), and despite its poverty, Kerala did manage to provide universal primary education and to run an effective system of universal health care, which contributed greatly to its having, by a big margin, the longest life expectancy in India and the lowest rates of infant and child mortality, among its other health accomplishments.

In addition to these so-called 'social achievements', it was also clear even in those early days—despite the scorn I remember receiving from those who were opposed to the thesis of complementarity—that with the help of a more educated and more healthy work force, Kerala would also be able to grow faster in purely economic terms. After all, there are no influences as strong in raising the productivity of labour as health, education, and the cultivating of skill formation—a foundational connection to which Adam Smith, the father of modern economics, had given so much attention.

Now that the previously poor state of Kerala, with its universal health care and universal schooling, has the *highest* per capita income among all the states in India, it should be possible to see that there is real substance in the thesis of complementarity between economic growth and the advancement of human capability (particularly in the form of enhancing health care, education, and gender equity), with each reinforcing the other. Central to this understanding is the critical importance of social infrastructure in facilitating economic growth—a basic wisdom that made Kerala rise rapidly in economic terms, despite its policy mistakes in other spheres, which could—and should—have been corrected (to benefit even more from the foundational cultivation of the complementarity between the economic and the social).

The role of infrastructure—physical and social—in economic performance has been a neglected subject in policymaking in

India. The inattention to *physical* infrastructure (roads, power, etc.) is, however, receiving critical attention recently, largely driven by Gujarat's success in this field. This is certainly a good development and the importance of physical infrastructure is indeed an important recognition. But if wisdom is sensibly obtained from one experience—from a state that has done better than the rest of India and stands around being seventh in the league table of per-capita income and expenditure (as Gujarat does), then should not some wisdom be obtained also from the experience of another state which has lifted itself from being among the poorest in India to being the richest—at the very top of the league (as Kerala is now)?

A Final Word

If there is bad news about what is going on in India, there is also the possibility of good news. An independent and democratic country should be able to sort out its own problems. But we cannot do much without a clearer analysis of what has gone wrong—socially, economically, politically, and, no less importantly, culturally. In a small way the essays in this volume are attempts at helping to address many of the problems we face today. We need understanding as well as action, on many different fronts.

The penultimate essay, 'A Wish a Day for a Week', in this volume is the text of the opening address I was privileged to present at the Jaipur Literature Festival in January 2014. In line with a long-standing Indian tradition, I chose an allegorical form to make my points, planted into an imagined story. The points happen to relate to many of the major themes in this collection of essays. I hope the points survive even after the allegory fades.

I end with another story—an old one, all the way from the Vedas, about which I have said a few things earlier on in this introductory essay. The religion-minded reader of the Vedas may easily miss a thought-provoking verse in the form of a 'gambler's lament' in the *Rig Veda*. In this verse, a gambler recognizes that he should do useful things like cultivating land, rather than give in to his addiction to gambling. He notes, however, that despite his own reasoned decision not to gamble, he always ends up in gambling joints, thereby ruining his life. The verse is instructive and intellectually engaging—I believe this is the first discussion in the world of the now well-known philosophical problem of the 'weakness of will' (a problem that the ancient Greeks would study extensively under the name '*akrasia*')—a subject that is very important in contemporary philosophy as well.

The verse has another distinguishing feature that I thought was fun when I first read it in my school days. It is almost certainly the first invoking of a complaint about one's mother-in-law—very popular in medium-brow humour in the contemporary world. The Rig-Vedic gambler laments: "My mother-in-law hates me; my wife pushes me away."

There is surely a moral there, given the wide gulf between resolve and performance to which we Indians have got used. We need, first, a clear-headed understanding of what ails India most and have to identify the obstacles we must overcome to remove our ailments. And then, equally importantly, we have to do just that—what we have rightly resolved to do, and not follow the Rig-Vedic gambler in ending up somewhere else. Even the much-feared mother-in-law would then have reason to look kindly at us.

ailment = an often persistant bodily disorder

AMARTYA SEN
2015

INDIA THROUGH ITS CALENDARS

First appeared in *The Little Magazine: Other*, volume I, issue 1 (2000), pp. 4–12.

"The calendar," argued Meghnad Saha, the distinguished scientist and the leader of calendar reforms in India, "is an indispensable requisite of modern civilized life." He could have gone further than that. The need for a calendar has been strongly felt—and well understood—well before the modern age. The calendar, in one form or another, has been an indispensable requisite of civilized life for a very long time indeed. This explains why so many calendars are so very old, and also why most civilizations, historically, have given birth to one or more specific calendars of their own. The multiplicity of calendars *within* a country and within a culture (broadly defined) has tended to relate to the disparate preoccupations and concerns of different groups that coexist in a country.

Calendars as Clues to Society and Culture

The study of calendars and their history, usage, and social associations can provide a fruitful understanding of important aspects of a country and its cultures. For example, since calendars often have religious roles, there is sometimes a clear connection between regional religions and domestic calendars. Indeed, even the global calendars of the world are often classified as 'Christian', 'Muslim', 'Buddhist', and so on. The connection between calendars and cultures, however, goes well beyond this elementary linkage. Since the construction of calendars requires the use of mathematics as well as astronomy, and since the functioning and utilization of calendars involves cultural sophistication and urbanity, the history of calendrical progress can tell us a lot about the society in which these developments occur.

Furthermore, given the fact that local times vary with the exact location of each place within a country, the use of a shared time and a common calendar requires the fixing of a reference location (such as Greenwich for Britain) and a principal meridian (in the case of Britain, the one that runs through Greenwich, giving us the Greenwich Mean Time, the GMT). The determination of a reference location and a principal meridian is also, if only implicitly, a political decision, requiring an integrated view of the country. When the GMT was imposed as the national standard in late nineteenth century Britain (the clinching statute came in 1880), it was not an uncontroversial decision: those in opposition included the Astronomer Royal, and also self-confident institutions that valued their independence and the 'accuracy' of their respective local times. The great clock of Christ Church in Oxford continued, for a while, to show, through an extra hand, both the GMT and its local time—5 minutes behind GMT—and the college tradition allowed the belief that 'one is not late till five minutes past the appointed time, that is till one is late by Oxford mean solar time as well as Greenwich.'[1] When, in 1884, at the International Meridian Conference in Washington, DC, the meridian through Greenwich was given the status of being 'the prime meridian for all nations' (by which GMT also acquired its official international position), Britain's dominant standing in world affairs certainly played an important political part.

Because of these associations, the nature, form, and usage of calendars in a particular society can teach us a great deal about its politics, culture, and religion as well as its science and mathematics. This applies even to as diverse a country as India, and it is in this sense that there will be an attempt in this essay to try to understand India through its calendars.

Millennial Occasions and Akbar's Concerns

In fact, this is a particularly apt moment to undertake an exercise of this kind. The second millennium in the Gregorian calendar, which is now extensively used in India as well, is at its end. In one system of counting, the Gregorian second millennium will end on 31 December 2000, but the glittering celebrations that have already occurred on 31 December 1999, indicate that the other view—according to which we are already in the third millennium—has its devoted supporters, at least among the fun-loving world population.

Even though the divisions of time that any particular calendar gives are quite arbitrary and dependent on pure convention, nevertheless a socially devised celebratory break point in time can be an appropriate occasion for reflection on the nature of the world in which we live. Indeed, this is a particularly good moment to re-examine the Indian calendars themselves to interpret the nature of this country, since this is a subject of a great deal of internal debating right at this time. Different ways of seeing India—from purely Hinduism-centred views to intensely secular interpretations—are competing with each other for attention.

It is worth recollecting in this context that a little over 400 years ago when the first millennium in the Muslim Hijri calendar was completed (the year 1000 of the Hijri era ran from 9 October 1591 to 27 September 1592), Emperor Akbar was engaged in a similar—but very much grander—exercise in the Muslim-dominated but deeply multireligious India. Akbar's championing of religious tolerance is, of course, very well-known, and is rightly seen as providing one of the major building blocks of Indian secularism. But, in addition, Akbar's actions and policies also related closely to his inquiries and interpretations of India, and in that investigation, the calendrical systems had an important place.

Indeed, Akbar tried to understand the different calendars known and used in India, along with trying to study the different religions practised in the country. He went on, in the last decade of the millennium (in fact, in 992 Hijri, corresponding to 1584 AD), to propose a synthetic calendar for the country as a whole, the 'Tarikh-Ilahi', just as he also proposed an amalgamated religion, the 'Din-Ilahi', drawing on the different religions that existed in India. Neither of these two innovations survived, but the motivations behind the two moves—interrelated as they are—have received attention over the centuries and remain very relevant today. The present millennial occasion may well be an appropriate moment to return to some of Akbar's questions and concerns, presented at the end of a different millennium.

To this, I shall return at the end of the essay. But, first, I must examine the principal calendars that have governed the lives of Indians, and try to use that information for whatever understanding of India it offers. This perspective can provide

clues to many different aspects of science and society of India
as well as its cultures and practices.

The Indian Calendars

India provides an astonishing variety of calendrical systems,
with respective histories that stretch over several thousand
years. The official Calendar Reform Committee, appointed in
1952 (shortly after Indian independence), which was chaired
by Meghnad Saha himself, identified more than thirty well-
developed calendars in systematic use in the country.[2] These
distinct calendars relate to the diverse but interrelated histories
of the communities, localities, traditions, and religions that
have coexisted in India. If one wanted confirmation of the pervasive pluralism of India, the calendars of India would provide
fine evidence in that direction.

The authoritative *Whitaker's Almanac* reduces this long list
to seven principal 'Indian eras'. It also gives the translation of
the Gregorian year 2000 into these selected major calendars.
Since, however, the beginning of the year in different calendars
occur at different times and in different seasons (for example,
the Saka era, the most widely used indigenous calendar in
India, begins in spring, in the middle of April), these translations have to be seen in terms of substantial overlap rather than
full congruence. The Gregorian year 2000 AD corresponds,
Whitaker's Almanac reports, respectively with:

- Year 6001 in the Kaliyuga calendar;
- Year 2544 in the Buddha Nirvana calendar;

- Year 2057 in the Vikram Samvat calendar;
- Year 1922 in the Saka calendar;
- Year 1921 (shown in terms of 5-yearly cycles) of the Vedanga Jyotisha calendar;
- Year 1407 in the Bengali San calendar;
- Year 1176 in the Kollam calendar.

To this list, we can, of course, add other major calendars in extensive use in India, including the old Mahavira Nirvana calendar associated with Jainism (in use for about the same length of time as the Buddha Nirvana calendar), and later additions, such as the Islamic Hijri, the Parsee calendar, and various versions of Christian date systems (and also the Judaic calendar, in local use in Kerala, since the arrival of Jews in India, shortly after the fall of Jerusalem).

Ancient India and Its Calendars

It is clear from the table of Indian calendars in *Whitaker's Almanac* that the Kaliyuga calendar is apparently much older than—and quite out of line with—the other surviving old calendars. It also has a somewhat special standing because of its linkage with the religious account of the history of the world, described with mathematical—if mind-boggling—precision. (It is the last and the shortest of the four *yugas*, meant to last for 432,000 years, and has been preceded respectively by three other *yugas*, which were in length—going backwards—two, three, and four times as long as the Kaliyuga, making up a total of 4,320,000 years altogether.) It is, of course, true that the Vikram Samvat and the Saka calendar are also sometimes called 'Hindu calendars', and they are almost invariably listed under that heading, for example, in *The Oxford Companion to the Year*. But they are mainly secular calendrical systems that were devised and used—for all purposes including *inter alia* religious ones—by people who happened to be Hindus. In contrast, Kaliyuga is given an orthodox and primordial religious status. Furthermore, as the ancientness of Hinduism is not in doubt, and since ancient India in often seen as primarily Hindu India, the temporal seniority of the Kaliyuga has also acquired a political significance of its own, which has a bearing in the interpretation of India as a country and as a civilization.

Interesting enough, according to *Whitaker's Almanac*, Kaliyuga too, like the Gregorian, is at the end of a millennium—its sixth. This 'double millennium' seems to offer cause for some jollity (such coincidences do not occur that often), not to mention the opportunity of inexpensive chauvinism for Indians to celebrate the completion of a sixth millennium at about the same time that the upstart Europeans enjoy the end of their modest second millennium.

How authentic is this dating of Kaliyuga in *Whitaker's Almanac*? The *Almanac* is quite right to report what is clearly the official date of Kaliyuga calendar. Indeed, that dating is quite widely used, and even the Calendar Reform Committee reported the same convention (noting that year 1954 AD was year 5055 in Kaliyuga, which does correspond exactly to 2000 AD being 6001 Kaliyuga). However, this numbering convention raises two distinct questions, which deserve scrutiny. First, does the official Kaliyuga date correspond to the 'zero point' of the analytical system of the Kaliyuga calendar?

Second, does the zero point of the Kaliyuga calendar reflect its actual historical age?

I fear I have to be the kill-joy who brings a doubly drab message. First, the zero point of Kaliyuga is not 6001 but 5101 years ago (corresponding to 3101–3102 BC). Second, this zero point (5101 years ago) is most unlikely to have been the actual date of origin of this calendar.

The first point is not in any kind of dispute, and the defenders of the pre-eminence of the Kaliyuga calendar rarely deny that the zero point is 3102 BC. The zero point can be easily worked out from a statement of Aryabhata, the great Indian mathematician and astronomer born in the fifth century, who had done some foundational work in astronomy and mathematics, particularly trigonometry, and had also proposed the diurnal motion of the earth (with a corresponding theory of gravity—later expounded by Brahmagupta in the sixth century—to explain why objects are not thrown out as the earth churns). He noted that 3600 years of the Kaliyuga calendar were just completed when he turned 23 (the year in which this precocious genius wrote his definitive mathematical treatise, known as *Aryabhatiya*).[3] That was the year 421 in the Saka calendar, which overlapped with 499 AD. From this it can be readily worked out that 2000 AD corresponds to year 5101 in the Kaliyuga calendar. This tallies also with what the Indian Calendar Reform Committee accepted, on the basis of all the evidence it had. This robs us of the opportunity of celebrating a double millennial occasion—the Gregorian second and the Kaliyuga sixth—but it still leaves the seniority of the Kaliyuga over the Gregorian quite unaffected, since 5101 years is quite long enough (at least for chauvinistic purposes).

It is, however, important to take note of the often-overlooked distinction between (1) a calendar's historical origin, and (2) its zero point as a scaling device. To illustrate the distinction, it may be pointed out that the zero point in the Christian calendar was, obviously, fixed later, not when Jesus Christ was born. The zero point of the Kaliyuga calendar is clear enough, but in itself it does not tell us when that calendrical system, including its zero point, was adopted.

It has been claimed that the origin (or year zero) in Kaliyuga was fixed by actual astronomical observation in India in 3102 BC. This has not only been stated by Indian traditionalists, it also received endorsement and support in the eighteenth century from no less an authority than the distinguished French astronomer Jean-Sylvain Bailly, who computed the orbit for Halley's Comet. But as the great scientist and mathematician Laplace showed, this hypothesis is not likely to be correct. There is a clear discrepancy between the alleged astronomical observations (as reported for the zero year) and what would have been seen in the sky in 3102 BC. Laplace had the benefit of contemporary astronomy to do this calculation quite precisely. This old calendar, ancient as it undoubtedly is, must not be taken, Laplace argued, as commemorating some actual astronomical observation.

The Indian Tables indicate a much more refined astronomy, but everything shows that it is not of an extremely remote antiquity ... The Indian Tables have two principal epochs, which go back, one to the year 3102, the other to the year 1491, before the Christian era ... Notwithstanding all the arguments brought forward with the interest he [Jean-Sylvain Bailly] so well knew how to bestow on subjects the most difficult, I am still of the opinion that this period [from 3102 BC to 1491 BC] was invested for the purpose of giving a common origin to all the motions of the heavenly bodies in the zodiac.[4]

Let me pause a little here to note two points of some general interest. First, Laplace is disputing here the astronomical claims—often made—as to what was actually observed in 3102 BC, and the critique is, thus, both of history (of the Kaliyuga calendar) and of applied astronomy (regarding what was observed and when). Second, Laplace does not treat the dating of 3102 BC as purely arbitrary. Rather, he gives it an analytical or mathematical status, as distinct from its astronomical standing. Backward extrapolation may be a bad way of doing history, but it is an exercise of some analytical interest of its own.

Indeed, Laplace can be interpreted as adding force to the view, which can receive support from other evidence as well, that it is mathematics rather than observational science to which ancient Indian intellectuals were inclined to give their best attention. From the arithmetic conundrums of the *Atharvaveda* and the numerical fascination of the epics to the grammatical tables of Panini and the numbering of sexual positions by Vatsyayana, there is a remarkable obsession in ancient India with enumeration and calculation. The plethora of Indian calendars and the analytical construction of their imagined history fit well into this reading of Indian intellectual tradition.

Returning to the Kaliyuga calendar, it is also perhaps of some significance that there is no corroboration of the use of the Kaliyuga calendar in the Vedas, which are generally taken to date from the second millennium BC. There is, in fact, plenty of calendrical discussions in the Vedas, and a clear exposition of a system in which each year consists of 12 months of 30 days, with a 13th (leap) month added every 5 years. While the oldest of the Vedas, the *Rigveda*, outlines the main divisions of the solar year into months and seasons (4 seasons of 90 days each), the more precise calculations, including the 'leap' (or intercalary) months can be found in the *Atharvaveda*.[5] But the exact accounting system used in the Kaliyuga calculations is not found anywhere in the Vedas—at least not in the versions that have come down to us. It appears that there is no overt or even covert reference to the Kaliyuga calendar in the Ramayana or the Mahabharata either. Consideration of this and other evidence even prompted Meghnad Saha and his collaborators in the Calendar Reform Committee to suggest that the Kaliyuga calendar might have taken its present form precisely at the time of Aryabhata, in 499 AD (indeed they speculated that its analytical system is 'a pure astronomical fiction created for facilitating Hindu astronomical calculations and was designed to be correct only for 499 AD,' p. 254).

This may or may not be exactly right, but it is difficult to escape the conclusion that the Kaliyuga has not been in use much longer—if at all longer—than other old Indian calendars. The Vikram Samvat calendar, which is quite widely used in north India and in Gujarat, is traced to the reign of King Vikramaditya, and has a zero point at 57 BC. But many of the accounts of the magnificent Vikramaditya are so shrouded in mystery, and there is so little firm evidence of its early use, that it is difficult to be sure of the exact history of the Vikram Samvat. In contrast, however, we do know that the Saka calendar, which has a zero point (not necessarily its historical origin) in 78 AD, was in good use by 499 AD. Indeed, we know from

Aryabhata's own dating of the Kaliyuga in terms of the Saka era (421st Saka year) that at least by then the Saka era is well known and in good use. While there is very little written evidence that survives on the use of the Saka calendar (or indeed any other old calendar), it is worth noting that the Badami inscription dating from 465 Saka era or 543 AD does confirm the use of the Saka era (not very long after the Aryabhata statement, dated at the 421st Saka year, or 499 AD).

It is hard to resist the conclusion that unlike what appears from the table in *Whitaker's Almanac*, the Kaliyuga is not a lone forerunner of all the other extant calendars. In fact, it is even possible that among the surviving calendars today, the Buddha Nirvana calendar (with a zero point in 544 BC) may actually be significantly older than the Kaliyuga calendar. And so, quite possibly, is the Mahavira Nirvana calendar of the Jains (with a zero point in 527 BC). While the first uses of these calendars are hard to identify, there is solid evidence of the use of the Buddha Nirvana calendar in Sri Lanka from the first century BC—earlier than any that point firmly to the use of the Kaliyuga calendar.

Since I have been quite critical of the claims of priority of the Kaliyuga calendar as an old Indian calendar, I should make a couple of clarificatory observations, to prevent misunderstandings. First, it is not my purpose to deny that the Kaliyuga calendar may have a very old lineage. There is much evidence that it draws on older Indian calendars, including those discussed in the Vedas. But this ancient Indian inheritance is shared also by the Buddha Nirvana calendar and the Mahavira Nirvana calendar. We have to remember that ancient India is not just Hindu India, and there is an ancestry that is shared by several different religions that had their origin or flowering in India. The often-repeated belief that India was a 'Hindu country' before Islam arrived is, of course, a pure illusion, and the calendrical story fits well into what we know from other fields of Indian history.

Second, even though the sensual pleasure of celebrating the completion of the sixth Indian millennium compared with the ending of the second Gregorian millennium may be denied to the Indian chauvinist, it is clear that by the time of the origin of Christianity, there were several calendars competing for attention in the subcontinent. What are now known as Christian calendars did not, of course, take that form until much later, but even the Roman calendars on which the Christian calendars (including the Gregorian) draw were going through formative stages over the first millennium BC, precisely when the inheritance of the old Indian calendars was also getting sorted out. There is indeed much give and take between the older civilizations over this period, and it is difficult to separate out what emerged through an indigenous process in the subcontinent—or anywhere else—from what was learnt by one culture from another.

There is evidence that Indians got quite a few of their ideas from the Greeks (there are several fairly explicit acknowledgements of that in the *Siddhantas*), as did the Romans, but then the Greeks too had insisted that they had received a number of ideas from Indian works. As Severus Sebokht, the Syrian bishop, said in 662 AD (in a different country, in a different context), "There are also others who know something." If the Kaliyuga calendar loses its pre-eminence in critical scrutiny, the temptations of national chauvinism does much worse (while Hindu chauvinism does worse still).

Variations and Solidarity

The immense variety of systematic calendars in India brings out an important aspect of the country, in particular its cultural and regional variation. And yet this can scarcely be the whole story, since despite this high variance, there is a concept of the country as a unit that has survived through history. To be sure, the presence of this concept is exactly what is denied in the often-repeated claim that India was no more than a large territory of small to medium fragments, united together, later on, by the cementing powers of British rule.

The British often see themselves as having 'authored' India, and this claim to imaginative creation fits well into Winston Churchill's belief that India had no greater unity than the Equator had. It is, however, of some significance that even those who see no pre-British unity in India have no great difficulty in generalizing about the quality of Indians as a people (even Churchill could not resist articulating his view that Indians were "the beastliest people in the world, next to the Germans"). Generalizations about Indians have gone on from the ancient days of Alexander the Great and Apollonius (an early 'India expert') to the 'medieval' days of Arab and Iranian visitors (who wrote so much about the land and the people) to the early modern days of Herder, Schlegel, Schelling, and Schopenhauer. It is also worth noting that an ambitious emperor—whether Chandragupta or Ashoka or Alauddin or Akbar—has tended to assume that the empire was not complete until the bulk of the country was under his rule. Obviously, we would not expect to see, historically, a pre-existing 'Indian nation' in the modern sense, waiting anxiously to leap into becoming a nation state, but it is difficult to miss the social and cultural linkages and identities that could serve as the basis of one.

To this much debated issue, we can ask, what does the calendrical perspective bring? The variety of calendars, divided not only by religious connections but also by regional diversity, seems to be deeply hostile to any view of Indian unity. However, it must be noted in this context that many of these calendars have strong similarities, in terms of months, and also the beginning of the year. For example, the Kaliyuga, the Vikram Samvat, the Saka, the Bengali San, and several other calendars begin very close to each other in the middle of April. There is evidence that their respective beginnings were typically fixed at the same point, the vernal equinox, from which they have moved over the long stretch of time in the last two millennia, during which the 'correction' for the integer value of the length of the year in terms of days has been slightly inadequate—again in much the same way.

The fact that the integer value of 365 days to the year is only approximate was, of course, known to the Indian mathematicians who constructed the calendars. To compensate for this, the periodic adjustment standardly used in many of the Indian calendars take the form of adding a leap or intercalary month (called a 'mala masa') to bring practice in line with the dictates of computation. But the adequacy of the correction depends on getting the length of the year exactly right, and this was difficult to do with the instruments and understanding at the time the respective calendars were initiated or reformed. Indeed, the sixth century mathematician Varahamihira gave 365.25875 days as the true measure of the year, which while close enough, was still slightly wrong, since the length of the sidereal year is 365.25636 days and the tropical year is 365.24220 days. The errors have moved the different north Indian calendars away from the intended fixed points, such as the vernal equinox, but they have tended to move together, with considerable solidarity with each other.

There are, of course, exceptions to this show of unity in slight error, since the south Indian calendars (such as the Kollam) and the lunar or luni-solar calendars (such as the Buddha Nirvana) follow different rules. Indeed, it would be hard to expect a dominant uniformity in the calendrical—or indeed cultural—variations within India, and what one has to look for is the interest that different users of distinct calendars have tended to have in the practices of each other. I shall argue later that this mutual interest extends also to the calendars used by Indian Muslims after Islam came to India.

One of the tests of the presence of a united perspective in calendrical terms, already discussed, is the identification of a principal meridian and a reference location (like Greenwich in Britain). It is remarkable how durable has been the position of the ancient city of Ujjayini (now known as Ujjain), the capital of several Hindu dynasties of India (and the home of many literary and cultural activities through the first millennium AD), as the reference location for many of the main Indian calendars. The Vikram Samvat calendar (with a zero point in 57 BC) apparently originated in this ancient capital city. But it is also the locational base of the Saka system (zero point in 78 AD) and a great many other Indian calendars. Indeed, even today, Ujjain's location is used to fix the anchor point of the Indian clock (serving, in this respect, as the Indian Greenwich). The Indian Standard Time that governs our lives still remains a close approximation of Ujjayini time—5 hours and 30 minutes ahead of GMT.

A contemporary visitor to this very modest and sleepy town may find it interesting to note that nearly two millennia ago, the well-known astronomical work *Paulisa Siddhanta*, which preceded the definitive *Aryabhatiya*, focused its attention on longitudes at three places in the world: Ujjain, Benares, and Alexandria. Ujjain serves as a good reminder of the relation between calendar and culture. We have wonderful descriptions of Ujjayini in Indian literature, particularly from Kalidasa in the fifth century, perhaps the greatest poet and dramatist in classical Sanskrit literature.

The elegance and beauty of Kalidasa's Ujjayini even made E.M. Forster take a trip there in 1914. Forster wanted to reconstruct in his mind what Ujjain looked like in the days that Kalidasa had so lovingly described. He recollected passages from Kalidasa, including the stirring account of evenings when 'women steal to their lovers' through 'darkness that a needle might divide'. But he could not get the old ruins there to reveal much, nor manage to get the local people to take the slightest interest in his historical and literary search. Ankle deep in the river Sipra, so romantically described by Kalidasa, Forster abandoned his search, and accepted the prevailing wisdom: "Old buildings are buildings, ruins are ruins."[6] I shall not speculate whether in that abandonment of historical exactness, there is something of a unity (perhaps illustrated even by the already discussed factual uncertainty of the Kaliyuga despite its mathematical exactness). But certainly there is something very striking about the constancy of Ujjain's dominance in Indian time accounting, even though the focus of political power, and of literary and cultural pre-eminence, shifted from Ujjain itself, a long time ago. Tradition can be a great ally of solidarity.

Interaction and Integration

One of the contrasts between the different Indian calendars relate to their respective religious associations. This was a matter of particular interest to that original multiculturalist, Akbar, as I have already discussed. He was especially concerned with the fact that as a Muslim he was ruling over a country of many different faiths. To that particular concern, I shall presently return, but I would like to clarify that even before the arrival of Islam in India, India was a quintessentially multicultural and multireligious country. Indeed, nearly all the major religions of the world (Hinduism, Christianity, Buddhism, Jainism, Judaism) were present in India well before the Muslim conquests occurred. The Indian civilization had not only produced Buddhism and Jainism (and later on, the Sikh religion as well), but India had the benefit of having Jews much longer than Europe, had been host to Christians two centuries before Britain had any, and provided a home to the Parsees right from the time when religious persecution began in Iran. In fact, Jews arrived shortly after the fall of Jerusalem, Christians appeared at least as early as the fourth century, and Parsees started arriving by the eighth. The different calendars associated with these religions—Buddhist, Jain, Judaic, Christian, Parsee—were already flourishing in India, along with the Hindu calendars, when the Muslim conquest of the north led to the influence of the Hijri calendar. Islam's arrival merely completed the picture of the comprehensive religious—and calendrical—diversity of India.

The pioneering multiculturalism of Akbar included his taking an interest in the religion and culture of each of these groups. In his 'House of Worship' (*Ibadat Khana*), the people from diverse religions who were encouraged to attend included—as Abul Fazl noted—not only the mainstream Hindu and Muslim philosophers (of different denominations), but also Christians, Jews, Parsees, Jains, and even members of the atheistic Charvaka school.

Akbar's attempt at introducing a combined calendar paralleled his interest in floating a combined religion, the Din-Ilahi. On the calendrical front, Akbar may have begun by just taking note of various calendars (Hindu, Parsee, Jain, Christian, and others), but he proceeded then to take the radical step of trying to devise a new synthetic one. In 992 Hijri (1584 AD, Gregorian), just short of the Hijri millennium, he promulgated the brand new calendar, namely, the Tarikh-Ilahi, God's calendar—no less. The zero year of Tarikh-Ilahi corresponds to 1556 AD (the year in which Akbar ascended to the throne), but that is not its year of origin. It was devised as a solar calendar (like the Hindu and Iranian/Parsee calendars of the region), but had some features of the Hijri as well, and also bore the mark of a person who knew the calendrical diversity represented by Christian, Jain, and other calendars in local use in Akbar's India. The Tarikh-Ilahi became the official calendar, and the decrees of the ruling Mughal emperor of India (the *farmans*) henceforth carried both the synthetic Tarikh and the Muslim Hijri date, and occasionally only the Tarikh.[7]

Even though Tarikh-Ilahi was introduced with a grand vision, its acceptance outside the Mughal court was rather limited, and the subcontinent went on using the Hijri as well as the older Indian calendars. While Akbar's constructive calendar died not long after he himself did, his various synthesizing efforts left a lasting mark on Indian history. But has the calendrical expression, in particular, of Akbar's synthesizing commitment been lost without trace?

Not so. There is a surviving calendar, the Bengali San, which was clearly influenced by Tarikh-Ilahi, and which still carries evidence of the integrating tendency that is so plentifully present in many other fields of Indian culture and tradition (such as music, painting, architecture, and so on). It is year 1407 now in the Bengali calendar, the San. What does 1407 stand for? Encouraged by Akbar's Tarikh-Ilahi, the Bengali calendar was also 'adjusted' as far as the numbering of year goes in the late sixteenth century. In fact, using the zero year of the Tarikh, 1556 AD (corresponding to year 963 in the Hijri calendar), the Bengali solar calendar, which has a procedure of reckoning that is very similar to the solar Saka system, was 'adjusted' to the lunar Hijri number, but not to the lunar counting system. That is, the 'clock' of the calendar was put back, as it were, from Saka 1478 to Hijri 963 in the newly devised Bengali San. However, since the Bengali San (like the Saka era) remained solar, the Hijri has marched ahead of the San, being a lunar calendar (with a mean length of 354 days 8 hours and 48 minutes per year), and the Bengali San—just turned 1407—has fallen behind Hijri as well.

Like the abortive Tarikh-Ilahi, the more successful Bengali San too is the result of a daring integrational effort, and its origin is clearly related to the synthetic experiment of the Tarikh-Ilahi (and thus, indirectly, to Akbar's multicultural philosophy). When a Bengali Hindu does religious ceremonies according to the local calendar, he or she may not be quite aware that the dates that are invoked in the calendrical accompaniment of the Hindu practices are attuned to commemorating Mohammad's journey from Mecca to Medina, albeit in a mixed lunar–solar representation.

The tradition of multiculturalism in India is particularly worth recollecting at this moment in Indian history, when India's secularism is being sporadically challenged by new forces of intolerance and by politically cultivated fanaticism of one kind or another. What is under attack is not only some 'modern' notion of secularism born and bred in post-Enlightenment Europe, or some quintessentially 'western' idea brought to India by the British, but a long tradition of making room for different cultures which had found many articulate expressions in India's past—partly illustrated by India's calendrical history as well.

Concluding Remarks

While I shall not try to summarize the essay, it may be useful to point to some of the main subjects with which this essay has been concerned. First, India does have a remarkable variety of well-developed calendars. They provide useful introductions to certain aspects of India's culture and society. In addition to discussing the principal Indian calendars, I have also tried to draw on their nature, origin, and history to try to understand the country in which they have been in use. Some of the conclusions have been quite firm: for example, the recognition that the allegedly ancient Kaliyuga calendar, in its developed form, is not older—possibly significantly younger—than the Saka calendar (or the Vikram Samvat), or some non-Hindu calendars such as the Buddha Nirvana or the Mahavira Nirvana.

Other conclusions, drawn on the calendric basis, are more conjectural, including the speculation that the traditional Indic culture has had much stronger attachment to mathematics and analytical reasoning than to observational science. This is no more than a tentative hypothesis, and at best, it suggests an elementary cultural question, rather than giving any kind of a firm answer. I must warn that I would certainly grumble if there were any attempt to link the recently emerging Indian dominance in computer software—or the manipulation of the Internet—as reflecting some kind of a millennia-old natural selection on the banks of the Kaveri or the Ganges! However, cultural—as opposed to genetic—predispositions remain interesting fields of investigation.

Second, while the variety of Indian calendars indicates how deeply pluralistic the country has been over many millennia (well before the arrival of Islam), the tendency towards solidarity is also well illustrated by the calendrical systems, and particularly by the consistent use of a principal meridian. Ujjain served as the reference location for Indian time two millennia ago, as it does today, in the form of the Indian Standard Time.

Third, the arrival of Islam and the dominance of Muslim rule have had a profound effect on India over the last millennium. But the consolidating tendency has continued, and it was given a particularly well-articulated form by Akbar, the Great Mughal. His integrating experiments, carried out in parallel in religion and in the calendrical system (respectively, through the Din-Ilahi and the Tarikh-Ilahi), may have been abortive, but the philosophy that they represented has had many integrative fruits. This is, of course, plentifully visible in Indian music, poetry, painting, and in other cultural fields, and all this relates indirectly to Akbar's attempt at calendrical unity which was a part of his general multicultural philosophy. As it happens, something of even the calendrical synthesis also survives in the form of the Bengali San—a legacy of the integrative effort initiated by Akbar.

Caught as we are in India today in conflicting attempts to interpret Indian civilization and society, the calendrical perspective offers, I believe, some insights that are relevant and forceful. The calendars reveal, in fact, a great deal more than just the months and the years.

Notes and References

1. See *The Oxford Companion to the Year*, eds Bonnie Blackburn and Leofranc Holford-Stevens (Oxford: Oxford University Press, 1999), p. 664.

2. See M.N. Saha and N.C. Lahiri, *History of the Calendar* (New Delhi: Council of Scientific and Industrial Research, 1992).

3. See Saha and Lahiri, *History of the Calendar* (1955), pp. 252–3; also S.N. Sen and K.S. Shukla, *History of Astronomy in India* (New Delhi: Indian National Science Academy, 1985), p. 298.

4. Marquis Pierre-Simon de Laplace, as quoted in W. Brennand, *Hindu Astronomy* (London, 1896), p. 31.

5. On this see O.P. Jaggi, *Indian Astronomy and Mathematics* (Delhi: Atma Ram, 1986), Chapter 1.

6. E.M. Forster, 'Nine Gems of Ujjain', in *Abinger Harvest* (Harmondsworth: Penguin Books, 1936, 1974), pp. 324–7.

7. See Irfan Habib (ed.) *Akbar and His India* (Delhi: Oxford University Press, 1997).

THE PLAY'S THE THING

First appeared in *The Little Magazine: Vox*, volume I, issue 5 (2000), pp. 4-9.

Injustice, inequality, poverty, hunger, tyranny, ignorance, exclusion, exploitation: there are many ailments that ravage the modern world. We have reason enough to be determined and resolute in fighting them. Such fights cannot escape being, in many ways, rather grim, since there are hard barriers to overcome. The bleakness of such fights also relates to the fact that we have to combat, often enough, forces that may be fiercely opposed to the necessary changes that can eradicate these intolerable phenomena.

However, there are many different ways in which injustice can be opposed. A bleak fight need not invariably take the form of grisly encounters. Play can be resistance as well. We have to appreciate the importance of the voice that play can give to people—even to the underdog—in their attempt to counter tyranny or exploitation or deep inequality.

Of course, play has many other attractions as well. We all know that. Fun and games can provide recreation; they can help us to stay healthy; they can stimulate our imagination; they can also give us ideas and visions. It has even been suggested by recent medical research that those who have a lot of fun tend to be less prone to sudden heart attacks (though it would be rather sad to seek fun primarily for that reason). G.K. Chesterton had a point when he remarked: "The true object of all human life is play. Earth is a task garden; heaven is a playground." This is surely right, but play can also do more than enrich our personal lives. We are watched in our play and this can be a way to make a point—indeed, even an effective point.

In fact, resisting injustice is only one of the uses of voice in play. Another is to express a fuller picture of people which can take us beyond the one-dimensional characterization of human beings that bigots—religious or political or whatever—try to peddle. For example, in the battle for the 'mantle' of ancient India (going back to the much invoked 'Vedic' heritage), which has become such an active part of our modern politics, it would be nice to know what these ancient people did when they were not busy chanting Vedic hymns. Their voice in play could give us a fuller image of what it was like to be in ancient India. Ovid noted that "in our play we reveal what kind of people we are". A play can be speech enough.

Our voice in play is, thus, an important and somewhat underexplored subject. In this essay I can briefly discuss only a few of the richly diverse aspects of play as voice. I begin with the role of play and voice in resisting oppression and inequality.

You Can't Be Serious!

Consider the tyrannical role that the House Un-American Activities Committee played in America, especially under the leadership of the mighty Senator Joseph McCarthy. This witch-hunting Committee had an astonishingly powerful role in undermining democracy and political liberty in America, in the guise of resisting Communism. Even though it gradually ran into opposition from powerful quarters (including, at one stage, even from the US Army), the Committee continued beyond Senator McCarthy's fall from grace, and despite a change in name, was not abolished until 1975. It took on new roles. The American protest movements against the war in Vietnam, during the 1960s and 1970s, gave room for much authoritarian harassment in the US.

One of the decisive as well as colourful moments in the diabolic life of the House Un-American Activities Committee was the appearance of Jerry Rubin and his 'co-conspirators', attired in fancy dress to disrupt the dignity of that august committee. The garments worn were quite outrageous—and funny. From that point onwards, it was hard to escape the sense of the ridiculous in the way that this glum Committee could be viewed, once that undermining had occurred. Rubin appeared in different clothing on different occasions—sometimes as a Viet Cong soldier (carrying a toy M-16 rifle), sometimes as Santa Claus, and once as Paul Revere, the great hero of the American war of independence. Rubin and other accused 'co-conspirators' turned this trial of 'the Chicago-7' into a theatre, and the public had enormous appetite for the latest in the daily drama.

The self-devised—and colourful—play gave Rubin and his 'co-conspirators' (such as Abbie Hoffman) a voice that the tyrannical Committee never intended to give them. Rubin and his friends made a different—but also important—point in their playful way when they tossed dollar bills from the balcony of the New York Stock Exchange. They were in the happy position to add injury to insult by giggling while stockbrokers suspended all trading to scramble for unearned money. The voice of play was loud and clear, making a comment on the otherwise invulnerable culture of commerce.

There is need for more recognition of the fact that play gives people—even the underdog—a voice, and the voice, however obtained, can be critically important for social rethinking. To be able to play with someone is to have a potential voice, even when that voice takes the form of a silent statement. Rubin and his friends knew that, and chose to 'redefine' a hearing into a game and grabbed a voice that the Committee could not deny them, given its determination to compel the 'conspirators' to come to the hearing.

Gentle undermining can indeed be an effective means of combat. There is an old story from Italy in the 1930s—from the days when resistance to fascism was continuing against the heaviest of odds. (I heard it from my late wife Eva Colorni, whose father was, in fact, shot and killed by the Fascist police in Rome, where he was editing the underground socialist paper, *Avanti.*) The story concerns a political recruiter from the Fascist Party trying to persuade a rural socialist that he should join the Fascist Party instead. "How can I," said the rural socialist, "join the Fascist Party? My father was a socialist. My grandfather was a socialist. I cannot really join the Fascist Party." The Fascist recruiter is exasperated by such a silly argument, devoid of political logic. "What kind of an argument is this?" he asks. "What would you have done, if your father had been, say, a murderer and your grandfather had been a murderer too? What would you have done then?" "Ah, then," said the rural socialist, "then, of course, I would have joined the Fascist Party."

The reply would not have maimed or crippled the Fascist recruiter, but the currency of the story—repeated to cheered audiences—could help to do some gentle but firm undermining of the party of tyranny. Amusement can be a potent means of fighting, and the determined introduction of play can do its bit for resisting tyranny.

The African American comedian, Dick Gregory, confided to his audience a great secret he knew about members of the Ku Klux Klan, the murderous racists who wear those elongated hats. "It is not widely known," he said, "that their heads are actually shaped like that." This must interest us all—good empiricists as we are—to look into the covers that conceal faces of tyranny to check their shapes. While that enjoyable contemplation does not do much to disable the racists, it does help to cut their standing down to size.

This is one of the reasons why visionary comedy and well-devised political cartoons can give powerful voice to the underdog. Charlie Chaplin was, of course, the acknowledged master of critical comedy. The portrayal of discomfiture of the worker on the production line in *Modern Times* was an eloquent speech, the radical message of which was intensified by the farcical absurdity of the idea that people could be expected to admire such vapid exercises in modernity.

This perspective calls for much wider use, and there is a connection here even with ancient Indian plays. As it happens, the feature of ridicule as a weapon has not yet received as much attention as it can sensibly get. Bhasa's *Daridracharudatta* or Shudraka's *Mrichchhakatika* may be rightly celebrated for the sceptical view of the wealthy and the powerful that they portray, and yet the portrayal is not just censorious, but also amusingly ridiculous. The corruption and misuse of power appear increasingly absurd in the light of avowal of high ideals. The revolutionary implications of these plays have indeed been noted, but the strategies used for creating discontent can be the subject of further literary examination.

Just in Jest

Returning to games and play (rather than theatre and plays), games that undermine authority are not invariably easy to arrange. And yet it is important to see clearly what would be gained if they could be devised or injected. Would we not like to see the powerful leaders of the Taliban in Afghanistan engage in playing games with the people over whom they rule, rather than going around covering women from head to toe and confiscating safety razors from heterodox men? A mixed doubles game of tennis may be a bit too much to expect, but even the stately game of chess, quite playable by silent and stationary women, would help to improve the souls of the Taliban leaders. Especially since, as Charles Dudley Warner remarked, "there is nothing that disgusts a man like getting beaten at chess by a woman". This surely, is creative disgust, and it can help to build a better world.

As was said earlier, play can also make other contributions. For example, they get people together. There has been increasing recognition of that amiable object of games, and its role in supplanting confrontation by congregation. The ancient Greeks knew this role well enough, and the Olympics were originally devised not just as events for displaying athletic excellence, but also as occasions for congenial meetings and friendlier contacts in contrast with combats in battlefields. In reviving the Olympics, and in other ways expanding occasions for game-related get-togethers, the contemporary world has given some acknowledgement to that ancient wisdom. Perhaps I should permit myself the parenthetic remark here that given our rate of success at the Olympic games, we Indians may have stronger reason than most to emphasize the 'get together' aspect of the Olympics over their 'win medals' aspect.

What's in a Game?

Resuming test matches between India and Pakistan, in either country, could certainly help to introduce a different dialogue between the two nations. Listening to each other on subjects other than Kashmir, intruders, nuclear bombs, and such could help a little in taking a less intense view of each other. This has its own value, especially at this time, even though it would do nothing to resolve the serious bones of contention between the respective governments, nor distract them from the deadly work of making nuclear bombs and placing them on missiles. I know that the nuclear adventures are often described as 'playing with fire', but that is a scandalous misuse of the word—a slander against the good name of play. It is not surprising that sectarian bigots on both sides have much against such test matches.

Indo-Pakistan relations, of course, have many special features, since in some ways we know each other well, even though our tendency to forget what we know in the heat of a dispute is quite extraordinary. In the context of many other disputes, suspicion of each other can be fed by mutual ignorance and non-communication. Games can help to make each nation or group see the humanity of others with somewhat greater clarity.

This can also be a big influence in the spread of science as well as culture across borders. Indeed, the dissemination of science, mathematics, and cultural contributions relates closely to viewing other cultures as having a human face and worthwhile involvements. For example, in discussing the spread of the decimal system of arithmetic from India, where it originated, to the Arab world (and then to the West), George Ifrah notes—in his book *From One to Zero*[1]—how the Arab interest in Indian pastimes played a collateral part. He quotes, for example, a medieval Arab poet from Baghdad called al-Sabhadi who theorized that there were "three things on which the Indian nation prided itself: its method of reckoning [the decimal system], the game of chess, and the book titled *Kalila wa Dimna* [a collection of legends and fables]". The spread of the art of decimal counting went hand in hand with a broader interest in the people involved, including the games they played and were proud to play.

People's tendency to amuse themselves and each other make them in some sense more human—more involved in constructive rather than destructive forms of living. The suspicions and apprehensions about people from other lands, from other cultures, often arise from knowing little about them, and insofar as anything is known about them, this takes, the form, frequently enough, of knowing only a little bit about only a few who may be involved in violence. In contrast, the knowledge of games that foreigners can participate in—and amuse themselves with—can come as a constructive recognition.

What we learn about each other in playing games with them need not of course be all positive and flattering. People do get overexcited about winning, lose their cool, cut corners of good behaviour, and some even cheat (with or without the help of match-fixers). And yet the totality of passions, warmth, and generosity, on the one hand, and competitiveness, excitability, and gamely cunning, on the other, reflect a rich picture of people as they are, and not as they would be seen through the prism of violence and homicide, which dominate the reporting of news of foreigners in the contemporary world. Blemishes may be imperfect, but they tend to dilute a little the kind of overriding suspicion and apprehension that standard news reporting seems to generate.

Gita Mehta has interpreted parts of contemporary India in terms of an analogy with snakes and ladders, which, like chess, is a game of Indian origin:

> The traditional Indian game of Snakes and Ladders is simple enough, played by rolling dice to determine how many squares a player may move his marker across the board, starting at square one and finishing at square one hundred. Because of its unpredictability it was one of our favourite games when we were children. There was the element of chance determined by the throw of dice. But more than that, the actual board was suggestive of danger, an austere geometry of squares broken by angled ladders and snakes with yawning jaws. Landing at the foot of the ladder meant you could climb it, sometimes moving thirty squares in a single throw. That was the good part. You could also make it all the way to square ninety-nine, only to encounter a snake painted in lurid colours. Then you had to slide down the serpent while your gleeful opponents streaked past.[2]

Gita Mehta's analogy with life in contemporary India works, I think, very well. It also helps the point about the closeness of play to life, so that knowing what games others play also has the effect of bringing us to a closer understanding of the lives they lead, and indeed the kind of people they are.

The Power of Folly

The voice of others that we hear in fun and games may often have weaknesses with which it is easy to sympathize. Indeed, a clear understanding of a person's weakness can greatly help to bring him or her out as a real human being. In the political revival of Hindu tradition that is being intensely cultivated in India at this time, the Vedas are getting a lot of adoration (often championed by people who have never read a line of Sanskrit). The Vedas are, of course, intensely interesting books, but we cannot begin to get any kind of idea of the people who were involved in the production of the Vedas if we stick only to the hymns and religious adulation. We have to look also at the conundrums that amused these fun-seeking people (*Atharvaveda* has many), even if we do not want to remind ourselves that the word 'Veda' has the same Indo-European root as the contemporary source of much diversion called the 'video'.

It is particularly worth taking some interest in the weaknesses of the Vedic people that make them human rather than unidimensional worshippers of godly entities. The first of the four Vedas, the *Rigveda*, has a major hymn dealing with the compulsive gambler. The gambler describes what a sorry pass he has come to. Among the troubles this man suffered, more than three thousand years ago, are the following: "My mother-in-law hates me; my wife pushes me away. In his defeat the gambler finds none to pity him. No one has use for the gambler; [I am] like an aged horse put up for sale."

The passionate man apparently had great difficulty in kicking the habit. The *Rigveda* quotes him reciting his vows, with reasoned explanation: "I will not gamble in the future, I am looked down upon by my friends." But then he goes on to confess that he still turns up at gambling joints, unable to resist: "I show up there like an adulteress visiting the appointed place." He ends with advice for the would-be gambler: "Do not play with dice. Cultivate your field and remain content with whatsoever you earn, thinking that as plenty."

Well, there is a lesson in all this, and the blemish of excessive gambling does not make this sufferer uniformly attractive. But it is also a human folly, not unknown in later times and in other countries.

Since imprudence unites rather than divides, this gives us an engaging—rather than distant (even alienating)—view of the Vedic people. It is also, I guess, a proof of the lasting power of folly that this anti-gambling verse in the *Rigveda* changed its role over the centuries and developed into something of an invocational verse at the beginning of gambling events, which preceded the throwing of dice. It was often recited by later gamblers in the belief that this would bring them good luck in gambling.[3] What began as an appeal to kick the habit ended up being a part of the habit itself.

We know about the continuing hold of dice in ancient India also from the story, known to every school child, of how the great Yudhisthira, in the Mahabharata, lost his kingdom in an irresponsible dice game. Again, this does not make Yudhisthira a nobler character, but it certainly makes this know-all and over-immaculate epic character a little more human and easier to sympathize with. That may not be much, but in the troubled world of mutual suspicion in which we live, we have reason to value such understanding of imperfect humanity.

No Epilogue

Voice is important in a variety of ways: in demanding redress, in arguing forcefully, in insulting nicely, and for conversing, colluding, and contradicting. It is crucial, in general, for interacting, and this includes making good use of democracy. It is right that most studies of voice deal with rather solemn applications. But fun and games also provide voice, and this can be important enough. As Rosalind says in *As You Like It*, "a good play needs no epilogue."

Voice in play can allow us to hear each other (breaking political silence) and to see each other in more flawed and accessible form (diluting an image of relentlessness). And most importantly, voice through play—even a unilaterally devised play—can give the underdog an opportunity that he or she may not otherwise have. We need our voice in play as much as we need it in our work.

Notes and References

1. George Ifrah, *From One to Zero* (New York: Viking, 1985).

2. Gita Mehta, *Snakes and Ladders: Glimpses of India* (New York: Nan A. Talese, Doubleday, 1997), pp. 15–16.

3. C. Panduranga Bhatta, *Dice-Play in Sanskrit Literature* (Delhi: Amar Prakashan, 1985), p. 1.

THE SMALLNESS THRUST
UPON US

This essay draws on Amartya Sen's address, 'The Idea of Social Identity', at the College de France in Paris, on 28 May 2001.

First appeared in *The Little Magazine: Belonging*, volume II, issue 3 (2001), pp. 6–12.

"There used to be a me," said Peter Sellers in a famous interview, "but I had it surgically removed." Removal is challenging enough, but no less radical is surgical addition—or implantation—of a 'real me' by others who propel us in the direction of a new view of ourselves. We are suddenly informed that we are not really what we took ourselves to be: not Yugoslavs, but actually Serbs ('You and I don't like Albanians'), or not just Rwandans, but Hutus ('We hate Tutsis'), or—as some of us old enough may remember from the 1940s—that we are not primarily Indians, or human beings, but in fact just Hindus or just Muslims (who must respectively confront Muslims, or Hindus, on the 'other' side). "Any kiddie in school can love like a fool," Ogden Nash had proclaimed. "But hating, my boy, is an art." That art is widely practised by skilled artists and instigators, and the weapon of choice is identity.

A great many of the contemporary political and social issues revolve around the conflicting claims of disparate identities, since the idea of 'belonging' and the conception of 'identity' tend to have far-reaching effects on our thinking about ourselves and about others.[1] A sense of identity can, of course, be a source of pride and of comfort, but it can also be the basis of irritation, hostility, and violence. We must ask some basic questions about the nature of identity.

A central feature of our self-conception has to be the inescapable plurality of our identities and the role that reasoning and scrutiny can potentially play in the choice of our identities. This recognition has to be contrasted with the contrary positions that—explicitly or by implication—dispute our freedom to choose. These are big debates even if they are very rarely discussed in an explicit form. The contentions can be illustrated with specific examples of what are, ultimately, identity battles. The two I would choose for discussion here are: (1) the often-presumed priorities of the 'communitarian' perspective (with the special privileging of a community-centred identity), and (2) the viewing of humanity solely in terms of 'nationalities' and seeing global issues in the narrower terms of 'international' issues (with the special privileging of our national identity). There are attempts here at imposing one specific identification as our pre-eminent identity over all others, and these attempts work towards eliminating choices that are central to our lives as thinking beings.

Our Diverse Diversities

Those who emphasize the importance of any specific identity (such as our community-based identity) tend to point out that ignoring these community-based diversities can be a very big loss for social analysis as well as practical ethics. This can indeed be the case, but we have to go much further than that in recognizing that we are not only diverse, but diverse in many different ways. Community competes with class, gender, political commitment, literary traditions, professional identities, social values, and many other sources of diversity. Even though exclusivity of one particular identity based on focusing on one specific source of diversity, is often presumed (typically implicitly), any claim of such exclusivity—even of predetermined priority—cannot but be altogether arbitrary.

We are all individually involved in identities of various kinds in disparate contexts, in our own respective lives. The same person can be of Malaysian origin, with Indian ancestry, a French citizen, a US resident, a Christian, a socialist, a woman, a poet, a vegetarian, a diabetic, an anthropologist, a university professor, an opponent of abortion, a birdwatcher, an astrologist, and also deeply committed to the view that creatures from outer space regularly visit the earth in colourful vehicles and sing cheerful songs. Each of these collectivities, to all of which this person belongs, gives him or her a particular identity, which can vary in importance in different contexts, and which can also compete with each other for this person's attention and loyalty when they have contrary bearings. There is no way of seeing a person as 'belonging' exclusively—or principally in a predetermined matter—to one group only. Each of these categories can be crucially important, in particular contexts. Reasoning can be critical in determining the relative importance of these diverse diversities, and in understanding the priorities between them, which may vary with circumstances. These choices cannot be settled—as some communitarians have claimed—as a matter of passive 'discovery'.[2]

Social Influences

Classifications can take many different forms, and not all of the categories that can be consistently generated can serve as a plausible basis for identity. Consider the set of people in the world who were born between 9 and 10 in the morning, local time. This is a distinct group, but it is hard to think that many people would get excited about the solidarity of such a group and the identity it can potentially produce. Similarly, people who wear size 8 shoes are typically not linked with each other with a strong sense of identity on that ground. Classification is cheap; identity is not.

In fact, whether a particular classification can plausibly generate a sense of identity or not must depend on social circumstances. For example, if size 8 shoes become very difficult to obtain for some complicated technological or business reason, then the need for shoes of that size may indeed become a shared predicament and can give reason enough for solidarity (in demanding change) and identity (in acting together in harmony). Similarly, if it were to emerge that people born between 9 and 10 am are, for reasons that we do not yet understand, particularly vulnerable to some specific ailment, then again there is a shared quandary which can provide a reason for a sense of identity. To consider a different variant of this example, if some authoritarian ruler wants to curb the freedom of people born in that particular hour, perhaps because of the ruler's supernatural belief on the perfidy of people born then (or because some Macbethian witches have told him that he will be killed by someone born between 9 and 10 am), then again a case for solidarity and identity may well emerge for the hapless targets of persecution.

Sometimes, a classification which is hard to justify intellectually may nevertheless be made important through social arrangements. Pierre Bourdieu has pointed out how a social action can end up "producing a difference when none existed," and "social magic can transform people by telling them that they are different": "That is what competitive examinations do (the 300th candidate is still something, the 301st is nothing). In other words, the social world constitutes differences by the mere fact of designing them."[3]

Even when a categorization is arbitrary or capricious, once they are articulated and recognized in terms of dividing lines, the groups thus classified acquire derivative relevance (in the case of the civil service examination, it may be between having a fine job or having none), and this can be a plausible enough basis for identities on both sides of the dividing line. The reasoning in the choice of relevant identities must, therefore, go well beyond the purely intellectual into contingent social significance. Not only is reason involved in the choice of identity, but it may particularly require some collateral social analysis of the grounds of relevance.

Reasoning is also important in the use of identity and the relative importance to be attached to different identities. We do have the opportunity to determine the weights we have reason to place on our different associations and distinct identities. When one has to do one thing or another, the loyalties can conflict between giving priority to, say, nationality, residence, race, religion, family, friendship, political commitments, professional obligations, or civic affiliations. We have to choose and decide, and the alternative to reflected choice is unreflected selection.

The Privileging of Community

I turn now to the importance of community and culture. They can undoubtedly be deeply important to us, and yet we have to distinguish that basic recognition from the adoption of a communitarian way of thinking. There is, of course, much that is attractive in communitarian thought, including the cultivation of responsibility towards other members of a shared community, and there is value even in the sense of 'warmth' and 'reciprocity' on which communitarians focus.

These issues can be quite momentous. In an eloquent passage, V.S. Naipaul brings out the seriousness of his worry about losing one's past—one's historical identity—as a result of the discipline of a homogenizing present. He illustrates the sense of loss with a concrete example in *A Turn in the South:*

> In 1961, when I was travelling in the Caribbean for my first travel book, I remember my shock, my feeling of taint and spiritual annihilation, when I saw some of the Indians of Martinique, and began to understand that they have been swamped by Martinique, that I had no means of sharing the world view of these people whose history at some stage had been like mine, but who now, racially and in other ways, had become something other.[4]

Concerns of this kind—in this case related to a shared history and a putative sense of community—are among the most powerful ideas that move people in the contemporary world.

However, focusing on one's community can also be a very limited and limiting perspective. This is not only because a community can be defined in many different ways (Naipaul's concern here is very different from a communitarian concern with, say, a religious community), but also because—no matter how defined—it has the effect of privileging one specific sense of identity over others, which too can be important. It can also encourage an indifferent attitude towards 'other people' who do not share with us that particular identity.[5] Communitarian thinking could have been a plausible supplement to universalist thoughts, but as a matter of fact, it has tended to replace other forms of analysis by vocal claims to the 'priority' of community. Indeed, the advocacy of communitarian perspectives has grown with a relentlessness that bears comparison with the progress of global warming and the depletion of the ozone layer.

In many versions of communitarian thinking, it is presumed—explicitly or by implication—that one's identity with one's community is the principal or dominant (perhaps even the only significant) identity a person has. This conclusion can be linked to two alternative—related but distinct—lines of reasoning. One line argues that a person, situated in a community and a culture, may not have access to other conceptions of identity and to other ways of thinking about affiliation. Their social background, firmly based on their 'community and culture', determines the feasible patterns of reasoning and conceptions, of ethics and of rationality that are available to them. The second line of argument does not anchor the conclusion to perceptual constraints, but to the claim that identity is a matter of discovery anyway, and the communitarian identity will be simply recognized to be of paramount importance.

Barriers of Culture

I begin with the argument from perceptual limitation, which can take the form of an amazingly strong assertion. In some of the more fervent versions, we are told that we cannot invoke any criterion of rational behaviour other than those that obtain in the community to which the person involved belongs. Any reference to rationality yields the retort, 'Which rationality?' or 'Whose rationality?' It is also argued not only that the *explanation* of a person's moral judgements must be based on the values and norms of the community to which the person belongs, but also that the *assessment* of these judgements can be done *only within* those local values and norms. This approach, which has drawn inspiration from some schools of anthropology (not necessarily with parental approval) has had the effect of rejecting intercultural normative judgements about behaviour and institutions, and sometimes even of denying the possibility of cross-cultural exchange and understanding. There is an insistence here on splitting up the large world into little islands that are not within intellectual or normative reach of each other.[6]

In fact, the so-called 'cultures' need not involve any *uniquely* defined set of attitudes and beliefs that can shape our reasoning, and indeed many of these 'cultures' contain very considerable internal variations. Different attitudes and beliefs may be entertained within the same broadly defined culture. Community and culture can, of course, have a strong influence on our thinking, but it can hardly rule out our ability, given the opportunity, to think 'differently'. If it actually did, what would be the need for the policing of adherence and loyalty, which is typically so active in communitarian activism, varying from book banning by fundamentalists to the monitoring of beards and headscarves by the Taliban authorities (or, for that matter, the draconian restrictions that are proposed for missionaries doing their respective advocacies in India)? There are various influences on our reasoning, and we need not lose our ability to consider other ways of reasoning just because of our community and culture.

Indeed, an expansion of the ability to make these choices freely can be seen to be an integral part of the phenomenon of what we call 'development'. This calls for necessary social, political, and economic changes, varying from the expansion and widening of educational opportunities to the enhancement of open public debates and dialogues, and the removal of handicaps of grinding poverty. It requires, among other things, the opportunity of exposure to other societies and other cultures, and at the same time, it demands that there be adequate opportunity—political, social, and economic—to have a fair understanding of one's own background (and not be overwhelmed by the global bombardment of commercial tides from abroad).

Cultural separatists are right to point out that one cannot reason from nowhere. But this does not imply that no matter what the antecedent associations of a person are, those associations must remain unchallenged, unrejectable, and permanent. The alternative to the 'discovery' view is not choice from positions 'unencumbered' with any identity (as some cultural polemicists seem to imply), but choices that continue to exist even in any *encumbered* position one happens to occupy. Choice does not require jumping out of nowhere into somewhere, but considering the possibility of moving from somewhere to somewhere else.

Identity Conflicts

I consider now the second way of privileging the communitarian identity, to wit, claiming that it must be seen to be preeminently peerless (even when we can understand the putative claims of other competing identities). But why so? The sense of belonging to a community, while strong enough in many cases, need not obliterate—or overwhelm—other associations, affiliations, and commitments. These choices are constantly faced (even though they may not be incessantly articulated).

Consider, for example, Derek Walcott's poem, 'A Far Cry from Africa', where he, situated in the Caribbean, notes the divergent pulls of his historical African background (his sense of association from where his ancestors came to the Caribbean) and his loyalty to the English language and the literary culture that goes with it (also, for him, a very strong association):

> Where shall I turn divided to the vein?
> I who have cursed
> The drunken officer of the British rule, how choose
> Between this Africa and the English tongue I love?
> Betray them both, or give back what they give?
> How can I face such slaughter and be cool?
> How can I turn from Africa and live?

Walcott cannot simply 'discover' his true identity; he has to decide what he should do, and how—and to what extent—to make room for the different loyalties in his life. We have to address the issue of conflict, real or imagined, and ask about the implications of our loyalty to divergent priorities and differentiated affinities. If Walcott wonders what conflict there is between his inseparable attachment to Africa and his love of the English language and his use of that language (indeed, his astonishingly beautiful and constructive use of that language), that points to broader questions of disparate pulls on one's life.[7]

The point at issue is not whether *any* identity whatever can be chosen (that would be an absurd claim), but whether we do have choices over alternative identities or combinations of identities, and perhaps more importantly, substantial freedom on what *priority* to give to the various identities that we may simultaneously have. A person's choice may be constrained by the recognition that she is, say, Jewish, but there is still a decision to be made by her regarding what importance to give to that particular identity over others that she may also have (related, for example, to her political beliefs, sense of nationality, humanist commitments, or professional attachments).

Nations, Persons, and Humanity

I turn, finally, to the privileging of nationality, and this can be just as limiting as the predetermined prioritization of community. If the world is 'partitioned' into different nations, and no person can view a member of a different nation except as the citizen of one country viewing a citizen of another, then inter-personal relations would be subsumed in international relations. This has a major bearing on our understanding of global justice, which has received much attention recently, partly as a result of the agitations about the world economic order and the protests associated with what is called 'globalization'. What bearing does the issue of identity have on that very large question?

The first distinction to make here is that between a broadly global perspective and a narrowly international one. While the importance of nationality and citizenship cannot be denied in the contemporary world, we also have to ask how we should take note of the relations between different people across borders tied to us by other identities (with solidarities based on classifications *other than* partitions according to nations and political units), such as political fellowship, cultural linkage, social beliefs, shared human concerns, bonds of shared deprivation (linked, for example, with class and gender), and other non-citizenal affiliations. How do we assess the demands of professional identities (such as being a doctor or an educator) and the imperatives they generate, without frontiers? These concerns, responsibilities, and obligations may not only be parasitic on national identities and international relations, they may also, often enough, run in contrary directions to international relations. Even the identity of being a 'human being', which is in a sense, our broadest identity, must have the effect, when given due consideration, of making us take note of a very wide viewpoint. The imperatives that we may associate with our shared humanity need not be mediated through our membership of collectivities such as 'nations' or 'citizenry'.

This can be a critically important recognition. The point is easy to see in the precarious subcontinent that is our home. We have reason enough to grasp the fact that people in India or Pakistan are not just citizens of these respective countries, but also human beings who can view each other as other human beings. We are not obliged to interrelate with each other only through our respective states or governments. Our precarious world—indeed our explosively nuclear world—demands (in the subcontinent and indeed elsewhere) that we ask ourselves who we are, and not just who we would be if our humanity were to be amputated, leaving us with only our nationality.

Globalization and Global Justice

These issues have become prominent in recent years for other reasons as well, for example, in the context of the challenges of globalization. The challenges have received attention at different levels, including in the noisy and rowdy form of protesting demonstrations—from Seattle and Melbourne and Washington to London and Prague and Quebec. One of the first features to note about the recent demonstrations against globalization is the extent to which these protests are themselves globalized events. To see them as 'anti-globalization' protests can be very misleading. They voice global discontent and disaffection, and draw on people from very many different countries and distinct regions in the world (the protesters are not the 'local boys' of Seattle or Quebec). And many of their values relate to global issues of inequality and disparity.

The concerns of the demonstrators are often reflected in roughly structured demands and crudely devised slogans, but the *themes* of these protests have been consistently more important than their *theses*. Their intense *questioning* has been more significant than the *ready-made answers* handed over in their slogans. The questions that emerge call for far-reaching institutional changes in global economic and political arrangements, varying from revision of patent laws and reciprocity in economic relations to the broadening of the institutional architecture we have inherited from the early efforts of the Bretton Woods agreements in 1944. These changes can actually involve greater, rather than less, globalized interactions. It is particularly important to see that the sense of identity which finds expression in these movements, and also in many other expressions of global concern (such as environmental agitations), goes well beyond national identities.

Identity choice has a strong bearing on global justice. Recognizing the possibility of identity choice has the immediate implication that global justice must be seen to be a much larger idea than international justice, with which it is often confused. To see global justice as international justice is to assume that the national identity of a person must somehow be our predominant identity. But people in different parts of the world interact with each other in many different ways—through commerce, science, literature, music, medicine, political agitations, and also through global NGOs, the news media, and so on. Their relations are not all mediated through governments or representatives of nations.

For example, a French feminist who wants to work towards remedying some features of women's disadvantage in, say, Sudan, draws on a sense of identity that does not operate through the sympathies of one nation for the predicament of another. Her identity as a fellow woman, or as a fellow human being with a commitment to gender equity, may be more important here than her citizenship. Similarly, many NGOs—Medecins Sans Frontieres, OXFAM, Amnesty International, Human Rights Watch, and others—explicitly focus on affiliations and associations that cut across national boundaries.

Reason or Surrender?

I end with trying to put a few issues in focus. First, we belong to very many different groups, and we have to choose our priorities between them. Even though the allegedly irresistible demands of a parochial identity—of a sect or a community or even a nation—may be invoked to bully us into submission, we have to resist smallness being thrust upon us.

Second, the communitarian identities may or may not be important for us, and it is for us to decide what importance to attach to them. That choice cannot be taken away from us on the basis of some supposed barrier of inscrutability, or some unreasoned belief in a predetermined priority.

Third, the world is not just a collection of nations, but also of persons. The relation between one human being and another need not be mediated by their respective governments. This can be a very important recognition in the precarious and insecure world in which we live, under the darkening shadow of missiles and nuclear bombs.

Fourth, international justice cannot exhaust the claims of global justice. Our global interrelations can be far more extensive than international interactions, and even anti-globalization protests cannot escape being global events. Questions of equity, concern, and responsibility have to be addressed in an adequately broad perspective.

To conclude, the implications of the plurality of identities and of the role of social reasoning and choice are, thus, immensely far-reaching. They have a direct bearing on a variety of critically important issues, varying from security to equity. We cannot hide away the questions we have to face and the choices we have to make by some arbitrary assumption of mutual incomprehensibility (allegedly due to the impenetrable barriers of culture). Nor can they be disposed of through some implausible conversion of the domain of reasoning into one of passive discovery. We have to take responsibility for the lives we lead, and even for the world in which we live. The alternative is not social wisdom but intellectual surrender.

Notes and References

1. I have tried to discuss the special issues raised by ideas of 'Indian identity' in my second Dorabji Tata Memorial Lecture, given in New Delhi on 26 February 2001. See 'The Indian Identity', in *The Argumentative Indian: Writings on Indian History, Culture and Identity* (London: Allen Lane, 2005).

2. For a forceful exposition of the 'discovery' view from the communitarian perspective, see Michael Sandel, *Liberalism and the Limits of Justice*, 2nd edition (Cambridge: Cambridge University Press, 1998), pp. 150–2.

3. Pierre Bourdieu, *Sociology in Question* (London: SAGE, 1993), pp. 160–1.

4. V.S. Naipaul, *A Turn in the South* (1989).

5. I have discussed some of these issues in the 2000 British Academy Lecture, 'Other People'. The full text is available at http://www.britac.ac.uk/events/archive/other_people.cfim.

6. I have discussed this issue in *Reason before Identity* (Oxford and New Delhi: Oxford University Press, 1999). It is also discussed at length in *Identity and Violence: The Illusion of Destiny* (New York: W.W. Norton and Company; and London and New Delhi: Penguin, 2007).

7. I have discussed the particular bearing of identity conflicts in Caribbean culture and politics in my Eric Williams Memorial Lecture, 'Identity and Justice', Trinidad, 23 March 2001. The lecture has been included in *The Face of Man, Volume 2: The Dr. Eric Williams Memorial Lectures 1993–2004* (Republic of Trinidad and Tobago: Central Bank of Trinidad and Tobago, n.d.).

HUNGER

Old Torments and New Blunders

First appeared in *The Little Magazine: Hunger*, volume II, issue 6 (2001), pp. 8–15.

"It is so old a story,/ Yet somehow always new," so said Heinrich Heine, the German poet, essayist, and political activist, in *Lyrisches Intermezzo*. That early nineteenth century frustration of Heine (*Intermezzo* was published in 1823—he went into voluntary exile in revolutionary Paris seven years later) cannot but recur in our thoughts as we observe the continued barbarity of old problems with new and added dimensions, in the distressing world in which we live. Nowhere, perhaps, is this as exasperating as in the terrible continuation of massive hunger and undernourishment in India.

It is not that nothing has been achieved in India over the half-century or more since Independence in 1947. Positive things have certainly happened. First, the rapid elimination of famines in India with Independence is an achievement of great importance (the last sizeable famine occurred in 1943—four years *before* Independence), and this is certainly an accomplishment that contrasts with the failure of many other developing countries to prevent famine. And yet this creditable record in famine prevention has not been matched by a similar success in eliminating the pervasive presence of endemic hunger that blights the lives of hundreds of millions of people in this country.

Second, the stagnating agriculture that so characterized—and plagued—pre-Independence India has been firmly replaced by a massive expansion of the production possibilities in Indian agriculture, through innovative departures. The technological limits have been widely expanded. What holds up Indian food consumption today is not any operational inability to produce more food, but a far-reaching failure to bring entitlement to food within the reach of the more deprived sections of the population. Indeed, as M.S. Swaminathan has pointed out, "We have reached a stage in our agricultural evolution when our production will increase only if we can improve consumption."[1]

First Enemy: Smugness and Ignorance

How can things be changed? The first thing to get rid of is the astonishing smugness about India's food record and the widespread ignorance that supports it. India has not, we must recognize unambiguously, done well in tackling the pervasive presence of persistent hunger. Not only are there persistent recurrences of severe hunger in particular regions (the fact that they don't grow into full-fledged famines does not arrest their local brutality), but there is also a gigantic prevalence of endemic hunger across much of India. Indeed, India does much worse in this respect than even Sub-Saharan Africa.[2] General undernourishment—what is sometimes called 'protein-energy malnutrition'—is nearly twice as high in India than in Sub-Saharan Africa. It is astonishing that despite the intermittent occurrence of famine in Africa, it too manages to ensure a much higher level of regular nourishment than does India. About half of all Indian children are, it appears, chronically undernourished, and more than half of all adult women suffer from anaemia. In maternal undernourishment as well as the incidence of underweight babies, and also in the frequency of cardiovascular diseases in later life (to which adults are particularly prone if nutritionally deprived in the womb), India's record is among the very worst in the world.

A striking feature of the persistence of this dreadful situation is not only that it continues to exist, but that the serious public attention it gets, when it gets any at all, is so badly divided.[3] Indeed, it is amazing to hear persistent repetition of the false belief that India has managed the challenge of hunger very well since Independence. This is based on a profound confusion between famine prevention, which is a simple achievement, and the avoidance of endemic undernourishment and hunger, which is a much more complex task. India has done worse than nearly every country in the world in the latter respect. There are, of course, many different ways of shooting oneself in the foot, but smugness based on ignorance is among the most effective.

Poverty, Health Care, and Education

This takes us to the next question. Once we get rid of the smugness, what should we do? The old barriers to good nutrition do, of course, remain and we have to recognize that they have not lost their bite. People have to go hungry if they do not have the means to buy enough food. Hunger is primarily a problem of general poverty, and thus overall economic growth and its distributional pattern cannot but be important in solving the hunger problem. It is particularly important to pay attention to employment opportunities, other ways of acquiring economic means, and also food prices, which influence people's ability to buy food, and thus affect the food entitlements they effectively enjoy.[4]

Further, since undernourishment is not only a cause of ill health, but can also result from it, attention has to be paid to health care in general and to the prevention of endemic diseases that prevent absorption of nutrients in particular. There is also plenty of evidence to indicate that lack of basic education too contributes to undernourishment, partly because knowledge and communication are important, but also because the ability to secure jobs and incomes is influenced by the level of education.

Maternal Undernourishment and Its Far-reaching Penalties

So low incomes, relatively higher prices, bad health care, and neglect of basic education can all be influential in causing and sustaining the extraordinary level of undernutrition in India. Yet, as Siddiq Osmani has shown, even after taking note of low levels of these variables, 'one would have expected a much higher level of nutritional achievement than what actually obtains' in India in particular, and in South Asia in general.[5] So something else must be brought in. Osmani suggests—plausibly enough—the lasting influence of maternal undernourishment, working its way via underweight babies (India and South Asia lead the world in this field), who grow into children and adults more prone to illnesses, of various kinds. This is in line with findings that have been identified by others, such as Ramalingaswami and his colleagues.[6] Recent medical research has brought out the long-run effects of foetal deprivation, reflected in low birth weight, which appear to cause immunological deficiencies and other health vulnerabilities. The health and nutritional adversity related to maternal undernutrition and low birth weight children is almost certainly a significant factor in explaining the terrible nutritional state of India.

Since material undernourishment is causally linked with gender bias against women in general in India, it appears that the penalty India pays by being unfair to women hits all Indians, boys as well as girls, and men as well as women. Even though there is ambiguous empirical evidence regarding the relative nutritional backwardness of girls vis-à-vis boys (as Svedberg discusses in his paper in this number), there is no dearth of definitive evidence of the neglect of pregnant women. For example, the proportion of pregnant women who suffer from anaemia—three quarters of all—is astoundingly higher in India than in the rest of the world. The long-run effects of underweight births not only worsen the chances of good health and nutrition of children—both boys and girls—but also immensely increase the incidence of cardiovascular diseases late in life.[7] Interestingly, since men are, in general, more susceptible to cardiovascular diseases, it also turns out that the adverse impact of the neglect of the nutrition of pregnant women is, in this respect, even greater for men than for women. What is sown in the form of unfairness to women is reaped as illfare of men, in addition to the suffering of women themselves.

The analysis so far has identified particular problems that have to be tackled if India is to overcome the massive prevalence of persistent hunger from which it suffers in many different ways. The areas of action include economic opportunities (such as growth of income and its distributional pattern), social facilities (such as basic health care and education), and the countering of special deprivations of women (such as material undernourishment). These are old problems that have not yet been overcome, unlike other fields in which success has been achieved, such as famine prevention and technological expansion of production opportunities. What, then, are the new problems?

Largest Food Mountains and Worst Undernourishment

The barriers to nutritional progress come not only from old dividing lines, but also from brand new ones. Sometimes the very institutions that have been designed to overcome old barriers have tended to act as reactionary influences in adding to inequity and unequal deprivation. The terrible combination that we have in India of immense food mountains on the one hand and the largest conglomeration of undernourished population in the world is one example of this.[8]

In 1998, stocks of food grains in the central government's reserve were around 18 million tons—close to the official 'buffer stock' norms needed to take care of possible fluctuations of production and supply. Since then, it has climbed and climbed, firmly surpassing the 50 million mark, and it appears, according to recent reports, that our stocks now amount to 62 million tons. To take Jean Drèze's graphic description, if all the sacks of grain were laid up in a row, this would stretch more than a million kilometres, taking us to the moon and back. Since Jean Drèze wrote this last year (2000), the stocks have risen some more, and the sacks would now take us to the moon and back to the earth, and then back to the moon again.

It is good to hear from the Government of India that a small part of this large stock will be used for various good purposes, including 1 million ton going for relief in Afghanistan (I applaud both as a human being and as the Honorary President of OXFAM, which is much involved in providing relief in Afghanistan), but this would neither make much of a dent in the good mountain, nor stop its relentless enlargement—perhaps to 75 million tons soon, or even to a 100 million.[9] The Food Minister has also proposed a different way of paying subsidies to the farmers, which apparently distributes them more equitably among the regions. Instead of the government's being obliged to buy food grains at the minimum support prices, food would now be sold at market prices and the government will pay the farmers the difference between the market prices and the minimum support prices. Farmers—even very big farmers—would no doubt be relieved to hear that their 'interests', as the expression goes, 'will be protected'. And, of course, the stocks will keep accumulating, even though they are now approaching four times the official 'buffer stock' requirements. And the public expense of the programme of subsidies (estimated not long ago at a staggering Rs 21,000 crore a year) is unlikely to spiral down. We are evidently determined to maintain, at heavy cost, India's unenviable combination of having the worst of undernourishment in the world and the largest unused food stocks on the globe.

Policy Delusions

What can be the explanation for this odd insistence on counterproductive policy? The immediate explanation is not hard to get. The accumulation of stocks results from the government's commitment to unrealistically high minimum support prices of food grains—of wheat and rice in particular. But a regime of high prices in general (despite a gap between procurement prices and consumers retail prices) both expands procurement and depresses demand. The bonanza for food producers and sellers is matched by the privation of food consumers. Since the biological need for food is not the same thing as the economic entitlement to food (that is, what people can afford to buy given their economic circumstances and the prevailing prices), the large stocks procured are hard to get rid of, despite rampant undernourishment across the country. The very price system that generates a massive supply keeps the hands—and the mouths—of the poorer consumers away from food.

But does the government not remedy this problem by subsidizing food prices according to the level of procurement prices—surely that should keep food prices low to consumers? Not quite. Jean Drèze and I discuss this issue more fully in our book, *India: Development and Participation*, but one big part of the story is simply the fact that much of the subsidy does in fact go to pay for the cost of maintaining a massively large stock of food grains, with a mammoth and unwieldy food administration (including the Food Corporation of India). Also, since the cutting edge of the price subsidy is to pay farmers to produce more and earn more, rather than to sell existing stocks to consumers at lower prices (that too happens, but only to a limited extent and to restricted groups), the overall effect of food subsidy is more spectacular in transferring money to farmers than in transferring food to the undernourished Indian consumers.

Need for a Clearer Class Analysis

If there were ever a case for radical class analysis, in which the left could take the right to the cleaners, one would have thought that this would be it. Sure enough, some public interest groups have protested and taken issues of fundamental rights to the Supreme Court. But the systematic criticism of this problem from the perspective of class inequality has been amazingly muffled and silent. The protest we hear is strangely divided, along with repetition of the *mantra* about keeping food prices high for the benefit of farmers and cultivators. Why is this so?

When the policy of food procurement was introduced and the case for purchasing food from farmers at high prices was established, various benefits were foreseen, and they are not altogether pointless, nor without some claim to equity. First, building up stocks to a certain point is useful for food security—even necessary for the prevention of famines. That would make it a good thing to have a large stock up to some limit—in today's conditions, perhaps even a stock of 20 million tons or so. The idea that since it is good to build up stocks as needed, it must be even better to build up even more stocks, is of course a costly mistake.

It is important in this context to also examine a second line of reasoning in defence of high food prices, which too comes in as a good idea and then turns counterproductive. Those who suffer from low food prices include some that are not affluent—the small farmer or peasant who sells a part of the crop. The interest of this group is mixed up with those of big farmers, and this produces a lethal confounding of food politics. While the powerful lobby of privileged famers presses for higher procurement prices and for public funds to be spent to keep them high, the interests of poorer farmers, who too benefit from the high prices, are championed by political groups that represent these non-affluent beneficiaries. Stories of the hardships of these people play a powerful part not only in the rhetoric in favour of high food prices, but also in the genuine conviction of many equity-oriented activists that this would help some very badly off people. And so it would, but of course it would help the rich farmers much more, and cater to their pressure groups, while the interests of the much larger number of people who buy food rather than sell it would be badly sacrificed.

There is need for more explicit analysis of the effects of these policies on the different classes, and in particular on the extreme underdogs of society who, along with their other deprivations (particularly low incomes, bad health care, inadequate opportunities of schooling), are also remarkably underfed and undernourished. For casual labourers, slum-dwellers, poor urban employees, migrant workers, rural artisans, rural non-farm workers, even farm workers who are paid cash wages, high food prices bite into what they can eat. The overall effect of the high food prices is to hit many of the worst-off members of society extremely hard. And while it does help some of the farm-based poor, the net effect is quite regressive on distribution. There is, of course, relentless political pressure from farmers' lobbies in the direction of high food prices, and the slightly muddied picture of some farm-based poor being benefited permits the confusion that high food prices constitute a pro-poor stance, when in overall effect it is very far from that.

It is said that a little knowledge can be a dangerous thing. So, unfortunately, is a little bit of equity when its championing

coincides with massive injustice to vast number of underprivileged people.

A Concluding Remark

Not only is the persistence of widespread undernourishment
in India—more than in all other regions in the world—quite
extraordinary, so is the silence with which it is tolerated, not to
mention the smugness with which it is sometimes dismissed.
Nutritional deficiencies affect the lives of Indians at different
ages but—as has been discussed—they can be closely interrelated. For example, the neglect of women's nutrition can work
through maternal undernourishment, foetal deprivation in the
uterus, low birth weights, undernutrition and ill-health of children, and ultimately morbidity of adults as well. Recent research
has brought out sharply the impact of early undernourishment
on long-run health, and even on the development of cognitive
functions and skills. The fact that India has such a massive
incidence of childhood undernourishment makes this a particularly alarming consideration. Indeed, the negative effects
of early undernourishment can be serious throughout one's
life, including in the propensity to suffer from cardiovascular
diseases in later ages (again, higher in India, controlling for
other influences, than almost anywhere else).

In battling against 'so old a story' of deprivation and hunger,
we also have to take note of the fact that the policy problems
can take forms that are 'somehow always new'. In addition
to addressing issues of economic growth and distribution, of
health care and basic education, and the very old problem of

gender bias and neglect of women's health, we must also reassess public policies based on explicit scrutiny of who benefits from the respective policies, and who—most emphatically—do not. Many of the underdogs of society face not only traditional problems that have kept them back, but also new adversities arising from public policies that are meant to help the underprivileged but end up doing something rather different.

Given our democratic system, nothing is as important as a clearer understanding of the causes of deprivation and the exact effects of alleged policy remedies that can be used. Public action includes not only what is done for the public by the state, but also what is done by the public for itself. It includes what people can do by demanding remedial action and through making governments accountable. I have argued in favour of a closer scrutiny of the class-specific implications of public policies that cost the earth and yet neglect—and sometimes worsen—the opportunities and interests of the underdogs of society. The case for protesting against the continuation of old disadvantages has been strong enough for a long time, but to that has to be added the further challenge of resisting new afflictions in the form of policies that are allegedly aimed at equity and do much to undermine just that. The case for relating public policy to a close scrutiny of its actual effects is certainly very strong, but the need to protest—to rage, to holler—is not any weaker.

Notes and References

1. M.S. Swaminathan, 'Bridging the Nutritional Divide: Building Community Centred Nutrition Security System', *The Little Magazine: Hunger*, volume II, issue 6 (2001).

2. On this see S.R. Osmani, 'Hunger in South Asia: A Study in Contradiction', and Peter Svedberg, 'Hunger in India: Facts and Challenges', both in *The Little Magazine: Hunger* (2001). See also Svedberg's *Poverty and Undernutrition: Theory, Measurement and Policy* (Oxford: Clarendon Press and Oxford University Press, 2000).

3. Jean Drèze and I discuss the role of inadequacy of public discussion in the formulation and persistence of faulty public policy in our joint book, Drèze and Sen, *India: Economic Development and Social Opportunity* (1995), and in the follow-up monograph, *India: Development and Participation* (New Delhi: Oxford University Press, 2002).

4. I have tried to discuss the basic issues in *Poverty and Famines: An Essay on Entitlement and Deprivation* (Oxford: Clarendon Press, 1981).

5. Osmani, 'Hunger in South Asia'. See also his 'Poverty and Nutrition in South Asia', First Abraham Horowitz Lecture, United Nations ACC/SNN, mimeographed, 1997.

6. V. Ramalingaswami, U. Jonssons, and J. Rohde, 'The Asian Engima', *The Progress of Nations 1996* (New York: UNICEF, 1996).

7. See particularly D.J.P. Barker, 'Intrauterine Growth Retardation and Adult Disease', *Current Obstetrics and Gynaecology*, volume 3 (1993); 'Foetal Origins of Coronary Heart Disease', *British Medical Journal*, volume 311 (1995); and *Mothers, Babies and Diseases in Later Life* (London: Churchill Livingstone, 1998). See also N.S. Scrimshaw, 'Nutrition and Health from Womb to Tomb', *Nutrition Today*, volume 31 (1996).

8. The discussion that follows draws on my Nehru Lecture, 'Class in India', given on 13 November 2001. See Amartya Sen, 'Class in India', in *The Argumentative Indian: Writings on Indian History, Culture and Identity* (London: Allen Lane, 2005).

9. M.S. Swaminathan, 'Using the Food Mountain', *The Hindu*, 10 November 2001; see also the editorial 'Resolving the Food Riddle' of the same day.

SPEAKING OF FREEDOM

Why Media Is Important for Economic
Development

This essay draws on a talk given at a joint meeting of the Caribbean Academy of Sciences and the University of West Indies, Trinidad, in March 2001, as well as on a keynote address at the General Assembly of the International Press Institute in New Delhi, given in January 2001.

First appeared in *The Little Magazine: Listen*, volume III, issue 3 (2002), pp. 9–16.

In a playful rhyme entitled 'Parliament Hill Fields', John Betjeman provides a fetching description of England:

> Think what our Nation stands for,
> Books from Boots and country lanes,
> Free speech, free passes, class distinction,
> Democracy and proper drains.

This diverse basket of good things reflects one view of England, at least a glimpse of the self-perception of the English—of England as seen by, and loved by, the English. There is affectionate familiarity, in addition to general plausibility, in this self-perception.

Freedom for Whom?

For those of us who grew up in the Empire rather than in the metropolis (the British Raj ended in India when I was approaching fourteen), we saw more of some of these virtues than of others. Class distinction, certainly, and even the occasional proper drain, and of course plenty of free passes for the loyalist of the regime. For the dissenters and practitioners of real free speech, the passes took them elsewhere. When I was in early and middle school, I was aware that three members of our extended family, including my uncle, were in prison.

They were there not because they had been convicted of anything, but they were held just as a 'precaution', under the Raj called 'preventive detention'. This was based on the presumption that they *could* do some political harm, if only in the form of some aggravating speech, had they been left free. Free speech and free choice of action did not have to be exercised to be penalised; an *anticipated* rebellious speech, or the *expectation* of a disloyal action, would qualify one for prolonged incarceration.

Democracy—so prized at home in Britain—was not quite on the list of goods to be exported to the colonies. Even when there was some tolerance of dissenting speech, the freedom to speak was at best extraordinarily fragile, which would break at the anticipation of a rough touch without actually having to be touched. In fact, free speech was just like 'free passes' (of which Betjeman speaks), which could be offered through discretion and promptly withdrawn at the first anticipation of what the Raj would identify as unhelpful indiscretion.

❧

The point of recollecting all this after more than half a century is not to grumble about the past, nor to point an accusing finger at the bosses of yesteryear. That would be a thoroughly pointless exercise. On the other hand, it is useful to recollect how hard it was to establish a claim to democracy and free speech in the very colonies of a country that had done so much to install democracy and free speech in the world. The English were right to be proud of their own practice of free speech and of their determination to resist challenges to democracy at home (no matter how tight-fisted they might have been in distributing these goods abroad). And by the same token, the people of India and other former colonies, who had to stand up for—and often fight for—democracy and for the protection of free speech in their countries, sometimes against severe adversities, have reason enough to prize what they now have. This is worth recollecting precisely because these hard-earned gains are often not adequately appreciated and valued. Free speech, in particular, still remains a relatively scarce commodity in the world, and the importance of free speech deserves serious discussion in the contemporary world.

Freedom as a Universal Value

The recognition of the universal value of free speech and political freedom in general is still relatively new in the world as a whole. It is a quintessential product of the twentieth century. The emergence of free speech and democratic values does, of course, have a long history—not least in England. But the universality of these values is still quite new and greatly in need of critical appreciation and defence. The rebels who forced restraint on the king of England through the Magna Carta saw their case to be a purely local one; it was for England in particular. The American fighters for independence as well as French revolutionaries contributed greatly to the understanding of the need for democracy as a general system. And yet the focus of their practical demands was still quite local, confined in effect to the two sides of the north Atlantic, founded on the special economic, social and political history of the region—of the old 'West'. African Americans were not even a part of the system of freedom that the democratic revolutionaries demanded for Americans, and many things far more severe than taxation went altogether without representation in the American republic that overthrew British rule.

Indeed, throughout the nineteenth century, theorists of democracy and defenders of free speech found it quite natural to discuss whether one country or another was yet 'fit for democracy'. That changed only in the twentieth century, with the recognition that the question itself was wrong: a people does not have to be judged to be fit *for* democracy, rather it has to become fit *through* democracy. This is a momentous transformation, covering the contemporary world with billions of people, and with varying history and culture and diversity of affluence.[1]

Freedom and Development

How does the value of democracy and of free speech relate to the challenges of development? This is the subject of this essay. Is free speech in competition with economic and social development? Or are they complementary, and if so how? Or, going further, is free speech a part—a constituent part—of development? These issues have to be discussed, and not least by economists, of which I am one.

I think the first claim to record is that development cannot really be seen merely as the process of increasing inanimate objects of convenience, such as raising the GNP per head, or promoting industrialization or technological advance or social modernization. These accomplishments are, of course, valuable—often crucially important—but their value must depend on what they do to the lives and freedoms of the people involved. For adult human beings, with responsibility for choice, the focus must ultimately be on whether they have the freedom to do what they have reason to value. In this sense, development consists of expansion of people's freedom.

The second point to note is that freedom of speech is indeed a very important part of human freedom. To be able to speak to each other, to hear one another, cannot but be a central capability that we human beings have great reason to value. This is primarily because, as Aristotle had noted long ago, we are socially interactive creatures, the fulfilment of whose lives requires the ability to associate, converse, and socialize with others—with people at home and abroad. Speech is, thus, a part of human life, and free speech a basic part of human freedom.

In addition to the intrinsic importance of free speech, it also has instrumental roles and even some constructive importance. I must, of course, discuss them for a more complete picture of the role of free speech in human development. But it is best to acknowledge first the intrinsic importance of free speech so that this basic connection is not lost in the complex discussion of the instrumental and constructive functions of free speech. Even though, as I shall presently argue, the indirect contributions of free speech can be momentous, it is right to begin by noting that even in the absence of these indirect contributions, the direct and inherent importance of free speech in human life itself deserves adequate acknowledgement.

Freedom of the Press

Let me now turn to a substantive analysis of the diverse roles of free speech, and the connections that these roles have with the process of development. I shall begin by discussing perhaps the most critical as well as the most controverted part of free speech, to wit, the freedom of the press. Press freedom is indeed a central aspect of development.

But before I discuss the exact reasons for this valuation, I should begin with a word of caution. The press is not always an easy object to love. It is not, of course, hard to see why authoritarian rulers have reason—often very nasty reason—to hate the free press. And the ability and inclination of a free press to needle authoritarian rulers is certainly one part of the glory of the press.

However, frustration with the press is by no means confined only to dictators and potentates. There is the much-discussed issue of invasion of privacy by an unrestrained press, which can ruin many lives. No less important is the more common problem of being badly misreported. Indeed, when someone is wrongly reported in a newspaper, as happens from time to time, it can be extremely upsetting, since the false attributions typically communicate a lot faster and much more prominently than any subsequent corrections can. Anyone involved in public life would have reason enough to be concerned about the abuse of press freedom.

There is also a more serious reason—indeed a different type of reason—for grumbling about the media. Given the power of the press, it is easy for us to see how they can do a great deal of good to society. When that vital task is neglected, and the responsibility of public investigation is not seized, it can be very disconcerting. We have occasion enough to be disappointed at the unfulfilled promise of the free media and the corresponding loss of a potential benefit. This is a serious enough issue, and I shall come back to it presently.

What Does It Do?

We take up, first, the more positive side of press freedom. Why, we can ask, is the freedom of the press crucial for development? I think this is so for several distinct and basically separable reasons, and it is important to distinguish them clearly, so that we can adequately assess what is at stake. Indeed, we have to know what may be lost when censorship is imposed and press freedom is suppressed. Lord Northcliffe may have been right to grumble nearly a hundred years ago, "The power of the press is very great, but not so great as the power to *suppress*." But we have to understand what the world loses as a result of authoritarian exercise of the power to suppress.

Press freedom is, I would argue, important for development for at least four distinct reasons:

- **Intrinsic value** of speech and public communication, which are inescapably linked with the relevance of press freedom;
- **Informational functions** of a free press in disseminating knowledge and facilitating critical scrutiny;
- **Protective roles** of press freedom in giving voice to the neglected and the disadvantaged, and thus helping the cause of greater human security; and

- **Constructive contributions** of free public discussion in generating ideas, in the formation of values, and in the emergence of shared public standards that are central to social justice.

I will discuss them in turn.

Intrinsic Value of Freedom

The assessment of development cannot be divorced from the lives that people can lead and the freedoms that they actually enjoy. I have tried to examine the plausibility of this claim in my book, *Development as Freedom*.[2] Development cannot be judged merely by the accumulation of inanimate objects of use, such as a rise of the gross national product (GNP) or technological progress. For responsible human beings, the focus must ultimately be on whether they have the freedom to do what they have reason to value. This makes freedom the central object of development, and given that basic recognition, it is easy to see that freedom of speech and communication must be among the constitutive ingredient of development—an important component of developmental ends.

Freedom of speech, in this perspective, does not have to be justified by its indirect effects, but can be seen to be part and parcel of what we value and have reason to value. It must, therefore, figure directly in any accounting of development. The absence of a free press and the suppression of people's ability to speak to—and communicate with—each other directly impoverishes human freedom and impairs development, even if the authoritarian country that imposes this suppression happens to have a high GNP per head or have accumulated a large mass of physical wealth.

Informational Role of the Press

I turn now to the informational function of the press—a part of its instrumental role. This function relates not only to specialized reporting (for example, on scientific advances or on cultural innovations), but also to keeping people generally informed on what is going on where. Furthermore, investigative journalism can also unearth information that would have otherwise gone unnoticed or even unknown. All this is so obvious that I hardly need elaborate.

I shall presently discuss the protective function of press freedom in giving people a hearing and a voice. But in the context of the present discussion of the informational role of a free press, let me comment that rapid dissemination of information can also make a contribution to protection and security. Consider, for example, the Chinese famine of 1958–61, in which between 23 to 30 million people died. Despite the fact that the Chinese government was quite committed to eliminating hunger in the country, it did not substantially revise its disastrous policies (associated with the ill-advised Great Leap Forward) during the three famine years. This was possible because of the lack of a political opposition and absence of an independent critique from the media (on which more presently), but the Chinese government itself did not see the need to change its policies partly because it did not have enough information on the extent to which the Great Leap Forward had failed.

Because of the absence of an uncensored press and other modes of public communication, local officials across China were under the impression that while they themselves had failed, the other regions had done well. This gave incentive to each local unit—collectives or communes in various formations—to concoct their agricultural data to pretend that they too were doing well enough. The totality of these reported numbers vastly inflated the Chinese government's own estimate of the total amount of food grains that the country had. Indeed, it led the Chinese central authorities, at the peak of the famine, to the mistaken belief that they had 100 million metric tons more of grain than they actually had.

The information that is lost as a result of censorship of the press by an authoritarian government can devastatingly mislead that government itself. I do not wish to make the press more swollen-headed than it already is, by invoking William Cowper and saying that the press, like God, "moves in a mysterious way/ His wonders to perform." But whether or not the press is swollen-headed, it is certainly true that censorship of the press can not only help to keep the citizens in the dark, it can also starve the government itself of vitally important information.

Confrontation and Security

I turn now to the confrontational role of the press in giving the government the political incentive to respond to the needs of the people. The rulers have the incentive to listen to what people want if they have to face their criticism and seek their support in elections. It is, thus, not at all astonishing that no substantial famine has ever occurred in any independent country with a democratic form of government and a relatively free press. The Chinese famine of 1958–61 could decimate tens of millions of people over three years without leading to a rapid policy revision not just because the government had wrong information (itself connected, as I have just argued, with press censorship), but also because people were kept in the dark about the crises and the mortality, and since no newspaper was allowed to criticize the government.

A similar story can be seen in other major famines, whether we consider the Soviet famines of the 1930s, or the Cambodian famines of the 1970s, or the famines under African military dictatorships in the last three decades, or in Sudan or North Korea in the very recent past, not to mention the famines under colonial rule. Indeed, the Bengal famine of 1943, which I witnessed as a child, was made possible not only by a lack of democracy, but also by severe restrictions on the local press on reporting and criticism. The disaster received attention in Britain, from where India was governed, only after Ian Stephens, the courageous editor of *The Statesman* of Calcutta (then British-owned) decided to break ranks by publishing graphic accounts and stinging editorials on 14 and 16 October 1943. This was immediately followed on 18 October by a *mea culpa* letter on the size of the death toll by the Governor of Bengal to the Secretary of State for India in London, followed by further confessions of *culpas* in the subsequent days, followed by heated parliamentary discussions in Westminster, and followed ultimately by the beginning—at last—of public relief arrangements the following month, when the famine, which had already killed millions, ended.

The protective role of the press needs recognition and emphasis. When things are routinely good and smooth, the sheltering role of a free press and the related democratic freedoms are typically not desperately missed. But they come into their own when things get fouled up, for one reason or another. The recent problems of East and Southeast Asia bring out, among many other things, the penalty of limiting democratic freedom, of which press freedom is a part. Indeed, when the financial crisis in this region (from 1997 onwards) led to a general economic recession, the protective power of democratic freedoms—not unlike that which prevents famines—was badly missed in some countries in the region. Those who were newly dispossessed often did not have the voice they needed. The victims in, say, Indonesia or South Korea—the unemployed or those newly made economically redundant—may or may not have taken very great interest in democratic freedoms when things had been going up and up together for all. But when things came tumbling down and divided they fell (as people standardly do in any large economic decline), the lack of democratic institutions including a free press tended to keep their voices muffled and ineffective. Not surprisingly, civil and democratic rights, including a free press, became part of the demands on which the recent agitations and rebellions have focused, and there has already been remarkable progress in political and civil rights in several countries in East and Southeast Asia (including, of course, South Korea and Indonesia).

Constructive Role and Value Formation

I turn now to the fourth reason for the centrality of press freedom, along with other democratic and civil rights. Informed
and unregimented *formation* of our values requires openness of
communication and arguments, and the freedom of the press
cannot but be crucial to this process. Indeed, value formation
is an interactive process, and the press has a major role in
making these interactions possible. As new standards emerge
(for example, the norm of smaller families and less frequent
childbearing), it is public discussion as well as proximate emu-
lation that spread the new norms across a region and ultimately
between regions.

Even the very concept of what is to count as a 'basic need'
tends to be dependent on public discussion on what is important, and no less importantly, on what is feasible. Human
beings suffer from miseries and deprivations of various kinds—
some more amenable to alleviation than others. The totality
of the human predicament would be an impossible basis for a
practical discussion of our 'basic needs'. Indeed, there are many
things that we might have good reason to value if they were feasible—such as complete immunity from illnesses of all kinds, or
even immortality. But we do not—indeed cannot—see them as
needs, precisely because we believe them to be infeasible. Our
conception of needs relates not only to the comprehension of
the nature and extent of deprivations, but also to our appreciation of what can or cannot be done about them. These evalu-
ations and understandings can be strongly influenced by the
freedom and vigour of public discussion. A free press can be a

great ally of the process of development through, among other connections, its constructive role in value formation.

Uses of Press Freedom

Before I end, let me come back to the postponed questions on limitations of practice that can make the press less effective and sometimes even less than benign in its social functioning. A criticism that is often made is that the newspapers may be far from neutral in their presentation. This need not, in itself, be a fatal flaw, so long as different newspapers present disparate points of view, and between them, give voice to many distinct perspectives that call for attention.

The problem, however, arises from the fact that given a systematic bias in the press, this may not actually happen. In this context, the private ownership of newspapers has often been seen, with reason, to be a source of concern, and there have also been suspicions, which too can be reasonable, about the selective influence of advertisers. Hannen Swaffer, the British journalist, said in frustration a quarter century ago: "Freedom of the press in Britain means freedom to print such of the proprietor's prejudices as the advertisers don't object to." That judgement is probably too cynical and unjustifiably harsh, but there are problems here, to which we must pay attention for better use of press freedom.

There is, in fact, no easy way of escaping the power of newspaper ownership. Newspaper establishments involve property, and it is hard to see that we can have arrangements through which newspaper owners own only that property—and no other. In dealing with this issue, public ownership may not help either, since that would give the ruling government a special power that would, to a great extent, defeat the purpose of the freedom of the press.

It is useful in this context to invoke the idea of what John Kenneth Galbraith has called 'countervailing powers'. What is needed is not so much to obliterate any particular power, but to confront one power with another. In the present context, this would be an argument not only for the multiplicity of private ownership from different parts of the business world, but also for supplementing them with cooperative ownership as well as with ownership by independent bodies and statutory boards. The presence of media other than newspapers, including radio, television, and the Internet, can also greatly help coverage and diversity. We have to rely, to a great extent, on the countervailing power of competition and confrontation to overcome the problem of bias.

There is also the different issue of the importance of journalistic ethics and commitment, which was briefly flagged earlier. This is not just a matter of the honesty and objectivity of journalism (though they too can be importantly involved), but also one of initiative, imagination, and special motivation which would be needed to break less travelled grounds. For example, even though it is very easy to be forceful on very visible deprivations such as a famine or severe unemployment, the importance of bringing less obvious adversities (such as non-extreme hunger or defective schooling arrangements) can also be very great. For example, while press freedom, along with other democratic freedoms, has certainly helped independent India to avoid major famines altogether in its entire half a century of existence (in contrast with what standardly happened in the British Raj), nevertheless less striking, but also important deprivations (such as endemic undernourishment, or persistent illiteracy, or inadequate health care) have not received the attention they deserve from the Indian press.

To overcome this, what is needed is not only a fuller practice of journalistic initiative and enterprise, but also the development of dedicated pressure groups that focus forcefully on particular deprivations. This too, in a broad sense, involves the invoking of countervailing powers to broaden the overall reach of the architecture of social institutions and activist alliances. There are examples of some success in a number of fields. For example, women's organizations and feminist groups in India have been able, in recent years, to give greater visibility and prominence to specific aspects of gender disparity, and have made a major contribution towards advancing public awareness and debate.

A Concluding Remark

So I conclude where I began. It is extremely important to see the critical importance of the freedom of the press in the process of development, but it is also necessary to seek ways and means of expanding its reach and securing its effective functioning, Press freedom does have several distinct and independently significant roles, including (1) its *intrinsic* importance as a constitutive part of development, (2) its *informational* function to broaden knowledge and understanding across the society, (3) its *protective* role in reducing human insecurity and in preventing serious deprivations, and (4) its *constructive* contribution in the interactive and informed formation of values.

However, none of these functions is mechanical or automatic. There is need for commitment, but also for an adequately broad institutional structure with ample countervailing powers to secure range and impartiality. Press freedom deserves our strongest support, but the press has obligations as well as entitlements. Indeed, the freedom of the press defines both a right and a duty, and we have good reason to stand up for both.

Notes and References

1. I have discussed these in my paper, 'Democracy as a Universal Value', *The Journal of Democracy*, volume 10, issue 3 (1999), pp. 3–17.

2. *Development as Freedom* (New York: Knopf; and Oxford: Oxford University Press, 1999).

SUNLIGHT AND OTHER FEARS

The Importance of School Education

First appeared in *The Little Magazine: Growing Up*, volume IV, issue 3 (2003), pp. 8–15.

Francis Bacon has observed that the child's fear of the dark is 'increased with tales'. He was drawing some kind of analogy here with people's exaggerated fear of death—the comparison occurs in a grim essay called 'Of Death'. Unfortunately, invented tales are not needed to drive fear into the minds of a great many children in the world. Fear of not just the dark night, but also of the sunlit day. There is much to fear in a day that begins without a meal, without a friendly school to go to along with other children, without relief from illnesses and maladies that are constantly present in a precarious childhood, and, not least, without anything much to look forward to in the future. Nothing brings out the poverty of India today as much as the state of many—indeed most—of our children.

The tragedy in all this lies not only in the bleakness of the real world in which Indian children live, but also in the fact that these deprivations are not hard to overcome, even within the means that India now has. Our children remain in the dire state in which they are mainly because of the lack of political and social engagement, not because of the lack of resources.

The Underfed and Undernourished

Consider the hunger of Indian children. Even though the famines of the British Empire disappeared rapidly enough in India with Independence, India's overall record in eliminating hunger and undernutrition, particularly of children, is quite terrible. Not only is there persistent recurrence of severe hunger in particular regions, but more amazingly, there is a dreadful prevalence of endemic hunger across much of India. Indeed, Indian children do far worse in this respect than do children even in famine-ridden Sub-Saharan Africa (as has been well discussed by Peter Svedberg in these pages).[1] Judged in terms of the usual standards of retardation in weight for age, the proportion of undernourished children in Africa is 20 to 40 per cent, whereas the percentage of undernourished Indian children is a gigantic 40 to 60 per cent. General undernourishment—what is sometimes called protein-energy malnutrition—is nearly twice as high in India as in Sub-Saharan Africa.

And yet, India has continued to amass extraordinarily large stocks of food grains in the central government's reserve. In 1998 the stock was around 18 million tons, which is just around the official 'buffer stock' norms that are adequate for protecting India from the vicissitudes of nature. However, since then the stocks have climbed and climbed, hovering between 50 to 70 million tons—food enough to fill sacks of grain that would stretch more than one million kilometres, taking us to the moon and back, and then some more. The stocks exceed 1 ton of food grains for every family below the poverty line. There is, of course, no plan to give it to them.

The government, we know, spends a very large sum of money to subsidize food prices. But to cut a long story short, subsidies can be used either to keep producer prices high (that is having elevated sale prices for the farmers who sell food to the government), or to make consumer prices low (reducing the prices at which the indigent Indian buyers can afford to buy food and feed themselves and their children). Political pressure of the farmers favours the former and they certainly have much more clout than the indigent consumers—and hungry Indian children—have (or can even dream of). The consequent regime of high food prices in general (that is, high procurement prices and high sale prices, even though the latter are lower than the former) both expands procurement and depresses demand. The odd price system, while generating a massive supply of food, also keeps the eager hands of Indian children away from the food. Stocks accumulate and remain large, and much of the 'food subsidy' goes to meet the cost of maintaining a massively large stock of food grains, with a gigantic food administration.

A thorough overhaul of India's food policy is needed right now, with hard-headed economic assessment of costs and benefits, including the unequal toll of placating farmers and also of bearing the cost of carrying unnecessarily large food stocks from one year to the next. That assessment must also include a humane understanding of why Indian children fear the morning light, with another hungry day to come.

The Unschooled and the Overlooked

What about schooling? India has many more children out of school than any other country. These statistics may not be seen as significant by some who would point to the fact that India is a large country. And so indeed it is. But China is larger still, with a much smaller—indeed a relatively tiny—number of children out of school. Also, even in proportionate terms, India does not do very much better than Africa in getting a high proportion of children to school. Bangladesh, which was much behind India, has been overtaking India recently.

Of course, the official statistics of school administration can provide some immediate comfort, since they claim that very few Indian children are unregistered in school. But these official statistics have never been reliable: the schools have built-in incentives to exaggerate school registration and to inflate attendance even more (by confounding registration with attendance, for example). Independent findings, such as the Census of India, or the National Sample Survey, still show that a significantly large proportion—about one out of five—of Indian children are not in school on a normal day. The regional pattern shows great asymmetry here, with nearly all children at school in states such as Kerala or Himachal Pradesh, while in other states like Uttar Pradesh or Rajasthan, a very high proportion of children are not there at all.

We certainly need to build many more schools. Also, we have to run them much better. These are serious needs. But the alleged lack of interest of parents in educating their children (particularly girls), which is often mentioned as a difficulty, is nothing quite like that. That alleged 'fact' is, of course, the oldest chestnut around, but all the probing empirical studies of this presumed phenomenon have brought out its falsity. The picture comes through particularly clearly in the most extensive study of Indian schooling problems done by the PROBE team (involving Jean Drèze, Anita Rampal, and many other dedicated investigators), and published in 1999.[2] It appears that not only do nearly all parents—across the regions—want their children (including girls) to go to school, but also a very high proportion (often more than 80 per cent of parents) want to make it obligatory for parents to send children to school (*if* a reliable school exists in the neighbourhood). This applies not only to those regions in which most children do go to schools, but also in those areas where children are very often not in school: the explanation of non-attendance has to be sought elsewhere.

The regional studies have also tended to confirm a similar picture. The first educational reports of the Pratichi Trust, which I was privileged to set up with the help of the Nobel award, also show how overwhelmingly anxious the parents in the surveyed region (mostly in West Bengal) are to send children—including girls—to school.[3]

The wrong diagnosis of parent reluctance is very unfortunate for several distinct reasons. The first is the long history of using this false diagnosis as an excuse that is given by governments to explain away their failure to do the duties of a decent state: a failure that is—more than any other factor—responsible for the problems of Indian school education in general and of girls' education in particular. Over the decades since Independence, one government after another—at the Centre and in the states—have referred to the alleged reluctance of parents as one big reason for the failure to get children, especially girls, to school. But as the PROBE report and indeed all other field studies bring out, there is very little general reluctance of parents to send all children—girls as well as boys—to school.

The explanation of non-attendance lies mainly elsewhere. The absence of schools that are conveniently close and proximate is one reason. Further, if having more schools is a crucial policy issue, so is generating the confidence of parents that their children, especially girls, would be safe in school (while the parents may be away at work in various activities, from till-ing land to carrying merchandise). Many of these schools are single-teacher schools, and the absenteeism of teachers is quite high in some areas, so that the parents cannot be sure, in many cases, that there would be someone to look after their children through the day. This can be a particularly serious fear in the case of girl children. To overlook the real and legitimate concerns of parents, and to blame instead the nastiness of parents, is a good way of adding a little insult to much injury.

Further, many schools have no lavatory facilities at all. Some do not have rooms either. In understanding why there is some parental reluctance to send their children to school in specific cases—even when in general the parents insist that they would like to send their children, including girls, to school—it is important not just to count the existence of schools, but also to go into the running of schools, involving physical facilities as well as teacher participation.

When I was a student myself, trying to learn some economics at Presidency College in Calcutta, I remember joining movements of schoolteachers who demanded some increase in their woefully low salaries. That was fifty years ago. With the new pay awards for public servants, the salaries of schoolteachers have risen enormously. Indeed, if one compares the relative differential between schoolteachers' salaries and the earnings of agricultural labourers, the differential in favour of the former has grown by leaps and bounds, and is now absolutely enormous. Some commentators object to raising this issue of relative pay: why should this comparison in particular be made? This is a good riposte, and there are indeed many other comparisons that can also be instructive. The immediate relevance of the teacher–labourer differential arises, however, from an economic consideration, and no less importantly, a fundamental social concern.

The economic issue relates to the cost of educating the children of the Indian underdog in rural as well as urban areas. The fact that in so-called 'alternative' schools—such as Sishu Siksha Kendras (SSKs) in West Bengal—it is possible to get qualified teachers with the same educational credentials at a fraction of the standard schoolteachers' salary in the public sector, indicates how the cost of educating the children of the Indian illiterate masses has been artificially raised. While there is much to be happy about in the fact that Indian school teachers now get a fine salary, the cost implications of expanding the reach of the school system also have to be taken into account.

Not surprisingly, many states (including West Bengal, Madhya Pradesh, and others) have gone increasingly in the direction of expanding 'alternative' schools, rather than having standard schools. The Pratichi Trust reports indicate that these alternative SSKs do no worse than standard schools. There may be some comfort in that (and the dedication of SSK teachers is often exemplary), but the alternative route cannot be a long-term solution, given the limited facilities of these alternative schools and the difficulty of expecting that the alternative system, with its *ad hoc* structure, can really become the principal mainstream for educating Indian schoolchildren. The SSKs are a plausible stopgap solution, but the basic issue of having an adequate number of standard schools—and being able to afford expansion—has to be addressed.

The social problem is no less immediate than the economic crunch. The Pratichi Education Report brings out how the parents of children from less privileged families feel neglected and ignored in the running of schools. Absenteeism of teachers is quite high in general, but it is outrageously large when the bulk of the students come from lower class backgrounds, with little income and less social status. There is a big 'class divide' between the poorer children and their families, on the one hand, and the well-paid teachers in the schools, on the other, who—as the studies suggest—often have little time for the underdog children.

The rapid increase in private tuition as a system for supplementing primary education that is offered in school not only shows how inadequate the school system has become, but also how the better-off can escape the penalties of bad schooling by spending money to get additional teaching for their own children. Use of private tuition for primary school children is virtually unknown outside India and South Asia: I had some difficulty in my conversations last year with educationists in China in explaining what exactly the phenomenon to which I referred was. They have never heard of primary education through private tuition! The evil of this unusual Indian arrangement consists not only of the inequity that it generates, but also its efficiency implications. Since rich parents do not suffer that much from the low quality of schools, given their ability to remedy the deficiencies through supplementary private tuition, they have far less interest in using their influence to make the schools run better.

The teachers' unions which have been extremely supportive of the teachers' right to a good salary as well as to their independence (and rightly so) must have a big role to play in advancing social justice and equity in India by improving the functioning of primary schools. There is also an important role for institutional reform, which can take the form—it has been suggested by the Pratichi team—of both insisting on having school-based parent–teacher committees (with effective representation of poorer and less privileged parents) and demanding that these committees have an operative voice in the running of schools and even perhaps in the renewal of budgetary allocations. Also, the system of school inspections, now defunct in many states, can be revived in an attempt to make the schools run better. If the hunger of Indian children, on which I commented earlier, is largely due to the inefficiency as well as inequity of public policy, there is a similar issue to be faced in addressing the illiteracy of Indian children.

Plural Benefits of Mid-day Meals

Similar issues can be raised about health care as well as medical delivery to the poorer Indians and to the Indian children who have had the misfortune of being born in less well-off families. Rather than trying to extend the analysis in that direction, let me probe further some of the issues already raised, and devote the rest of the essay to two specific questions about the schooling of Indian children. First, can the problem of hunger and undernourishment be tackled along with school education through such programmes as providing cooked mid-day meals in school? Second, why is schooling so important anyway for the future of Indian children?

Mid-day meals are not an Indian innovation. They have been used for centuries in Europe and elsewhere to make schools more attractive to children and to feed them better. There has been considerable public agitation lately to make cooked mid-day meals standardly available in all Indian schools. It is to the credit of the Supreme Court of India that it has recently spoken up in favour of the 'right' of Indian children not only to go to school, but also to have cooked mid-day meals there. Many states in India have argued that they do not have the funds to make this possible. There are indeed financial difficulties that several Indian states actually do face at this time. The big rise in public sector salaries, discussed earlier, which has a much wider coverage than the salaries of schoolteachers specifically, has certainly had a role in contributing to the relative insolvency of some states. To the extent that the Centre can help the states in this respect, there is a need to think about ways and means of cooperation in this tremendously important endeavour.

However, the states must also reexamine their commitments and priorities. Indeed, many states, with the pioneering example of Tamil Nadu, run good programmes of providing mid-day meals. Others, such as Rajasthan, are moving in that direction. There is no basic economic reason why all states cannot do this, if they decide that this is indeed one of their principal priorities. The question that does, however, arise is whether mid-day meals *should* be seen as being pre-eminently important, so that it acquires the status of an overwhelming priority. That case is not hard to establish. Cooked mid-day meals served in schools provide a number of interrelated and far-reaching benefits.

First, since Indian children suffer from exceptional under-nourishment, the possibility of reducing that deprivation through giving meals to every schoolchild has a strong case based on health grounds. The schools are an excellent point of delivery to those in greatest need. The loss of physical fitness and mental ability due to undernourishment in childhood is a major predicament of the Indian people, and the adversity can be dramatically reduced through school meals.

Second, school meals increase the attractiveness of going to school. It is not surprising that empirical studies have shown that attendance tends to be very favourably influenced by this provision. Feeding, in this sense, complements the effectiveness of the school system.

Third, the attention span of children from the poorer families is often severely restricted by the fact that they come to school on an empty stomach (the Pratichi team found how common the incidence was). Feeding not only supplements schooling, it can actually contribute to the effectiveness of the process of teaching.

Fourth, if school meals are served in the schools in cooked form, rather than students being given so-called 'dry rations', the gender bias in distribution within the family is avoided. It also appears that the provision of meals for schoolchildren also has a particularly favourable effect in releasing girls from family work to go to school.

Fifth, the experience of eating together in schools, without differentiation of caste, religion, class, or ethnicity, is also a contribution towards building a more united India. Being schooled together is itself an egalitarian experience, and eating together in schools can add greatly to promoting a non-discriminatory outlook.

As against that, those opposed to the mid-day meals point to several difficulties. The financial one has already been discussed and can certainly be overcome. There may, in addition, be organizational problems, particularly when the chosen food requires very heavy cooking (as seems to be the case with the grains used in Rajasthan), and apparently there is the possibility of illnesses resulting from corners being cut. These organizational problems demand serious investigation and engagement (including further scrutiny of the type of grains to use and whether less heavily cooked food may be nutritionally better anyway for the children). These problems have been surmounted in many states, and the others can overcome them too.

It is sometimes argued that schooling is concerned with educating, not with feeding, and that teachers do not have to supervise cooking. That argument takes an artificially fragmented view of the lives of children. Indeed, going further, it can be argued that not only the absenteeism of children, but also that of teachers can be reduced if providing regular school meals becomes the standard practice. In a school of the traditional type (with no meals), if a teacher does not show up, the children may suffer in the long run (education brings benefits over years, rather than over hours), but there may not be any great immediate discontent, if only because children—reasonably enough—love playing as well. On the other hand, if a child relies on having a cooked meal at the school, absenteeism has an immediately disquieting effect. The fact that absenteeism of staff at the schools may cause more protests under these circumstances may be an entirely positive influence in making the schools run in a more orderly way. Rather than 'disrupting' normal teaching (as is sometimes alleged), providing cooked school meals can add to the effectiveness of teaching through a lowered likelihood of the distressing phenomenon of teacher absenteeism.

What's the Point of Going to School?

I come now to the last question. What is so special about schooling? There has always been much scepticism about the value of formal school education in India, a scepticism to which even Mahatma Gandhi lent his voice. Indeed, sceptical questions about prioritizing school education are so often asked in India that there is a real contrast here with almost the whole of the rest of the world (from Japan, China, Korea, and Vietnam to France, Britain, USA, Brazil, and Cuba). So, at the risk of labouring the obvious, let me discuss what the point of schooling might be.

Indeed, the importance of school education is truly immense and many-sided. First, illiteracy and innumeracy are major deprivations—profound 'unfreedoms'—on their own. Not to be able to read, write, and count makes a person less free to have control over one's own life.

Second, basic education can be very important in helping people to get jobs and to have gainful employment. India has suffered greatly from the neglect of basic education, both in the domestic economy and in the reduced ability of the Indian masses to gain from the opportunities of global commerce. Whenever the educational opportunities have been good in India (like in high-level technical education and specialized skill formation), Indians—with the appropriate educational background—have been able to make superb use of the global facilities, but the need to extend that openness to basic education (and also to spread basic technical skills more widely) remains extremely strong.[4] India casts envious eyes on the recent economic successes of East and Southeast Asia and sees the opportunities of globalized trade writ large there. Those opportunities are indeed enormous, but to make good use of them, basic education of the population can be a greatly facilitating factor. This connection, while always present, is particularly critical in a rapidly globalizing world, in which quality control and production according to strict specification is critically important.

Third, schooling is not only an educational occasion, it is also a social opportunity to come out of one's home and to meet others, who come from different families, have dissimilar values and have knowledge of disparate walks of life. The discipline of schooling can also provide experiences of a very different kind from what one gets within the family. The education of the school-going child comes not only from the formal lessons, but also from the experience of schooling itself.

Fourth, when people are illiterate, their ability to understand and invoke their legal rights can be very limited. This can, for example, be a significant barrier for illiterate women to make use even of the rather limited rights that they do actually have. This was well established many years ago in a pioneering study by Salma Sobhan.[5] Lack of schooling can directly lead to insecurities by distancing the deprived from the ways and means of countering that deprivation.

Fifth, illiteracy can also muffle the political voice of the underdog and thus contribute directly to their insecurity. The connection between voice and security can well be very powerful: the observed fact that substantial famines do not occur in democracies is just one illustration of the effectiveness of political voice and participation. The enabling power of basic education in making people more effectively vocal has a significantly protective role and is, thus, central to human security.

Sixth, empirical work in recent years has brought out very clearly how the respect and regard for women's well-being are strongly influenced by such variables as women's ability to earn an independent income, to find employment outside the home, to have ownership rights, and to have literacy and be educated participants in decisions within and outside the family. Indeed, even the survival disadvantage of women compared with men in developing countries seems to go down sharply—and may even be eliminated—as progress is made in advancing the agency role of women.[6]

The different characteristics that favour a better situation for women (such as women's earning power, economic role outside the family, female literacy and education, women's property rights, and so on) may at first sight appear to be rather diverse and disparate, but what they all have in common is their positive contribution in adding force to women's voice and agency—through greater empowerment. The diverse variables identified in the literature, thus, have a unified strengthening role.

This role is of importance not only for women themselves, but can also have far-reaching impacts on the lives of all through its influence on the forces and organizing principles that govern decisions *within* the family. There is considerable evidence, for example, that fertility rates tend to go down sharply with greater empowerment of women. This is not surprising, since the lives that are most battered by the frequent bearing and rearing of children are those of young women, and anything that enhances their decisional power and increases the attention that their interests receive tend, in general, to prevent over-frequent child bearing. For example, in comparative studies of the different districts within India (done by Mamta Murthi and Jean Drèze), it emerges that women's education and women's employment are the two most important influences in reducing fertility rates.[7]

There is also much evidence that women's education and literacy tend to reduce the mortality rates of children. The influence works through many channels, but perhaps most immediately, it works through the importance that mothers typically attach to the welfare of the children, and the opportunity they have, when their agency is respected and empowered, to influence family decisions in that direction. Similarly, women's empowerment appears to have a strong influence (Murthi and Drèze provide evidence on this too) in reducing the much-observed gender-inequality in the survival of children (that is, in reducing the bias against young girls).

These connections between basic education of women and the power of women's agency are quite central to understanding the contribution of school education to human well-being and freedom. The removal of survival disadvantages of women (and of young girls in particular), the reduction of child mortality (irrespective of gender), and moderating influences on fertility rates are all among the basic issues involved in removing the downside risks that threaten life and dignity, and the schooling of girls can be a critically important vehicle for social change.

Finally, in addition to the provision of schooling, it is necessary to consider the coverage of education and the curriculum. The issues involved here include the importance of technical skill in our globalizing world, but there are also other matters involved, since schooling can be deeply influential in the identity of a person and the way we see each other. Recently, the perspective of clash of civilizations has gained much currency. What is most immediately divisive in this outlook is not the idea of the inevitability of a clash (that too, but it comes later), but the prior insistence on seeing human beings in terms of one—and exactly one—dimension only. To see people in terms of this allegedly pre-eminent and all-engulfing classification is itself a contribution to political insecurity.[8]

The issue has received attention, if only indirectly, in the context of the role of madrasas in the growth of fundamentalism in Pakistan and elsewhere, but there is a danger here from other sources as well, given the way cultural and educational narrowing is being advocated by some political groups in India. School texts have also been messed around to exaggerate and embellish a specifically 'Hindu' perspective in understanding the history of India. Well-known historical phenomena, important for India's exceptionally pluralist heritage (from the flourishing of the pre-Indo-European Indus Valley civilization to the absorption of wave after wave of new entrants), are being buried in political attempts to rewrite India's past. This is an ominous development. The importance of a good, non-sectarian curriculum can be quite central to the role of education in securing a better future for the children of India.

Like food, education is a source of nourishment. Indian children need not have their minds poisoned any more than they need to have their bodies famished, skills neglected, or potentials wasted. We have been shooting ourselves in the foot for a long time now—through our biased food policies, negligent educational efforts, inadequate health arrangements—and now there is also the curricular barbarism in schools that encourages us to shoot ourselves in the other foot. Indian children deserve better than that. They need daylight, not darkness, nor the fears that 'increase with tales'.

Notes and References

1. See Peter Svedberg, 'Hunger in India: Facts and Challenges', *The Little Magazine: Hunger*, volume II, issue 6 (November–December 2001).

2. *Public Report on Basic Education in India* (New Delhi: Oxford University Press, 1999).

3. *Pratichi Education Report I: The Delivery of Primary Education, A Study in West Bengal* (Delhi: TLM Books, 2002).

4. On this and related issues, see Jean Drèze and Amartya Sen, *India: Development and Participation* (New Delhi: Oxford University Press, 2002).

5. Salma Sobhan, *Legal Status of Women in Bangladesh* (Dhaka: Bangladesh Institute of Legal and International Affairs, 1978).

6. This is discussed in my essays 'Gender and Cooperative Conflict', in Irene Tinker (ed.), *Persistent Inequalities: Women and World Development* (Oxford University Press, 1990), and 'Missing Women', *British Medical Journal*, number 304 (March 1992).

7. See Mamta Murthi, Anne-Catherine Guio, and Jean Drèze, 'Mortality, Fertility and Gender Bias in India', *Population and Development Review*, number 21 (1995), and Jean Drèze and Mamta Murthi, 'Fertility, Education and Development: Evidence from India', *Population and Development Review*, number 27 (2001).

8. This problem is discussed in my essay 'The Smallness Thrust upon Us', included in this volume.

SHARING THE WORLD

Interdependence and Global Justice

This essay is based on the author's address at the General Assembly of the United Nations on 29 October 2004.

First appeared in *The Little Magazine: Globalisation*, volume V, issues 4 and 5 (2005), pp. 6–11.

J ustice, it has been argued, should not only be done, it must also be 'seen to be done'. Or, more explicitly (as Lord Hewart put it in his famous judgement in 1923), justice "should manifestly and undoubtedly be seen to be done". It is useful to think of this requirement of justice when assessing the pros and cons of globalization in general, and the particular role of interdependence in making globalization a success. There are good reasons to argue that economic globalization is an excellent overall goal and that it is making a very positive contribution in the contemporary world. At the same time, it is hard to deny that there is some difficulty in persuading a great many people—making them 'see'—that globalization is a manifest blessing for all, including the poorest. The existence of this confrontation does not make globalization a bad goal, but it requires us to examine the reasons for which there is difficulty in making everyone see that globalization is 'manifestly and undoubtedly' good.

The critical assessment of globalization has to go hand in hand with trying to understand why so many critics, who are not moved just by contrariness or obduracy, find it hard to accept that globalization is a great boon for the deprived people of the world. If many people, especially in the less prosperous countries in the world, have genuine difficulty in seeing that globalization is in their interest, then there is something seriously challenging in that non-meeting of minds. The underlying challenge involves the role of public reasoning and the need for what John Rawls, the philosopher, calls 'a public framework of thought', which provides 'an account of agreement in judgement among reasonable agents'. Rawls's own analysis of critical assessment was largely confined to issues of justice *within* a country, but it can be extended to global arguments as well, and certainly has to be so extended if we are trying to assess the ends, and also the ways and means, of appropriate globalization. The goal of globalization cannot be concerned only with commodity relations, while shunning the relations of minds.

Distribution of Benefits

When, a year ago, the General Assembly of the United Nations requested the Secretary-General to prepare a report on 'globalization and interdependence' to 'forge greater coherence', they were opening the door not only to conventional questions of ways and means, but also to questions that deal with the transparency of assessments and the discernability of benefits. We have to ask, in particular, how global economic relations may be assessed in a way that the consequent understanding can be widely shared.

Having started this essay at the level of some generality, let me now take a plunge in the interest of brevity to an exercise of assessment. The achievements of globalization are visibly impressive in many parts of the world. We can hardly fail to see that the global economy has brought prosperity to quite a few different areas on the globe. Pervasive poverty and 'nasty, brutish and short' lives dominated the world a few centuries ago, with only a few pockets of rare affluence. In overcoming that penury, extensive economic interrelations as well as the deployment of modern technology have been extremely influential and productive.

It is also not difficult to see that the economic predicament of the poor across the world cannot be reversed by withholding from them the great advantages of contemporary technology, the well-established efficiency of international trade and exchange, and the social as well as economic merits of living in open rather than closed societies. People from very deprived countries clamour for the fruits of modern technology (such as the use of newly invented medicines, for example, for treating AIDS); they seek greater access to the markets in the richer countries for a wide variety of commodities, from sugar to textiles; and they want more voice and attention from the rest of the world. If there is scepticism of the results of globalization, it is not because suffering humanity wants to withdraw into its shell.

In fact, the pre-eminent practical issues include the possibility of making good use of the remarkable benefits of economic connections, technological progress, and political opportunity in a way that pays adequate attention to the interests of the deprived and the underdog.[1] That is, I would argue, the constructive question that emerges from the anti-globalization movements. It is, ultimately, not a question of rubbishing global economic relations, but of making the benefits of globalization more fairly distributed.

How Fair Is the Share?

The distributional questions that figure so prominently in the rhetoric of both anti-globalization protesters and pro-globalization defenders need some clarification. Indeed, this central issue has suffered, I would argue, from the popularity of somewhat unfocused questions. For example, it is often argued that the poor are getting poorer. This, in fact, is by no means the standard situation (quite the contrary), even though there are some particular cases in which this has happened. Much depends, in any case, on what indicators of economic prosperity are chosen; the answers that emerge do not speak in one voice. Furthermore, the responsibility for failures does not lie only on the nature of global relations, and often enough relate more immediately and more strongly to the nature of domestic economic and social policies. Global economic relations can flourish with appropriate domestic policies, for example, through the expansion of basic education, health care, land reform, and facilities for credit (including micro-credit). These are good subjects for public discussion—for the exercise of minds—since economic understanding can be greatly hampered by uncritical and over-rapid attribution of alleged responsibility.

On the other side, enthusiasts for globalization in its contemporary form often invoke—and draw greatly on—their understanding that the poor in the world are typically getting less poor, not (as often alleged) more poor. Globalization, it is argued, cannot thus be unfair to the poor: they too benefit—so what's the problem? If the central relevance of this question were accepted, then the whole debate would turn on determining which side is right in this mainly empirical dispute: are the poor getting poorer or richer?

But is this the right question to ask? I would argue that it absolutely is not. Even if the poor were to get just a little richer, this need not imply that the poor are getting a *fair* share of the benefits of economic interrelations and of the vast potentials of globalization. Nor is it adequate to ask whether international inequality is getting marginally larger, or smaller. To rebel against the appalling poverty and the staggering inequalities that characterize the contemporary world, or to protest against unfair sharing of the benefits of global cooperation, it is not necessary to show that the inequality is not only very large, but it is also getting larger.

The central questions have been clouded far too often by over-intense debates on side issues (to which both sides in the dispute have contributed). When there are gains from cooperation, there can be many alternative arrangements that benefit each party compared with no cooperation. It is necessary, therefore, to ask whether the distribution of gains is *fair* or *acceptable*, and not just whether there *exist* some gains for all parties (which can be the case for a great many alternative arrangements). As J.F. Nash, the mathematician and game theorist, discussed more than half a century ago (in a paper from *Econometrica* 1950, which was among his writings that were cited by the Royal Swedish Academy in awarding him the Nobel Prize in economics), the central issue is not whether a particular arrangement is better for all than no cooperation at all (there can be many such alternatives), but whether the particular divisions to emerge are fair divisions, given the alternative arrangements that can be made.[2] The criticism that a distributional arrangement from cooperation is unfair cannot be rebutted by just noting that all the parties are better off than would be the case in the absence of cooperation: there can be many—indeed infinitely many—such arrangements and the real exercise is the choice *among* these various alternatives.

The Phantom Chase

I can try to illustrate the point with an analogy. To argue that a particularly unequal and sexist family arrangement is unfair, it does not have to be shown that women would have done comparatively better had there been no families at all. That is not the issue: the bone of contention is whether the sharing of benefits within the family system is seriously unequal in the existing institutional arrangements. The consideration on which many of the debates on globalization have concentrated, to wit, whether the poor too benefit from the established economic order, is inadequately probing—indeed it is ultimately the wrong question to ask. What has to be asked instead is whether they can feasibly have a fairer deal, with a less unequal distribution of economic, social, and political opportunities, and if so, through what international and domestic arrangements. That is where the real issues lie.

This is also why the so-called 'anti-globalization' protesters, who seek a better deal for the underdogs of the world economy, cannot be sensibly seen—contrary to their own rhetoric—as being really anti-globalization. Their search has to be for a fairer deal, a more just distribution of opportunities in a modified global order. And that is also why there is no real contradiction in the fact that the so-called 'anti-globalization protests' are now among the most globalized events in the contemporary world. It is a global solution they must ultimately seek, not just local withdrawals.

But can the deal that different groups get from globalized economic and social relations be changed without busting or undermining these relations altogether, and in particular without destroying the global market economy? The answer, I would argue, is entirely in the affirmative. Indeed, the use of the market economy is consistent with many different ownership patterns, resource availabilities, social opportunities, rules of operation (such as patent laws, anti-trust regulations, etc.). And depending on these conditions, the market economy itself would generate different prices, terms of trade, income distributions, and more generally diverse overall outcomes. The arrangements for social security and other public interventions can make further modifications to the outcomes of the market processes. Together, they can radically alter the prevailing levels of inequality and poverty. All this does not require a demolition of the market economy, but does demand alternations of the economic and social conditions that help to determine what market solutions would emerge.

The central question is not—indeed cannot be—whether or not to use the market economy. That shallow question is easy to answer, since it is impossible to achieve much economic prosperity without making extensive use of the opportunities of exchange and specialization that market relations offer. Even though the operation of the market economy can be significantly defective (for example, because of asymmetric—and more generally imperfect—information), which must be taken into account in making public policy, nevertheless there is no way of dispensing with the institution of markets in general as an engine of economic progress. Using markets is like speaking prose—much depends on what prose we choose to speak.

The market economy does not work alone in globalized relations—indeed it cannot operate alone even *within* a given country. It is not only the case that a market-inclusive overall system can generate very distinct and different results depending on various enabling conditions (such as how physical resources are distributed, how human resources are developed, what rules of business relations prevail, what social security arrangements are in place, and so on), but also these enabling conditions themselves depend critically on economic, social, and political institutions that operate nationally and globally. As has been amply established in empirical studies, the nature of market outcomes is massively influenced by public policies in education, epidemiology, land reform, micro-credit facilities, appropriate legal protections, etc., and in each of these fields there are things to be done through public action that can radically alter the outcome of local and global economic relations. It is this class of interdependencies which we have to invoke and utilize to achieve greater prosperity, more equity and fuller security.

Indeed, there can be a very positive role for the critical voice that the protest movements provide, but the voice has to aim at real problems not phantom ones. It is certainly true that global capitalism is typically much more concerned with expanding the domain of market relations than with, say, establishing democracy, or expanding elementary education, or enhancing social opportunities of the underdogs of society. Mere globalization of markets, on its own, can be a very inadequate approach to world prosperity. In keeping that recognition constantly in focus, scrutiny, and protest can play a constructive part.

Sharing Global Justice

The injustices that characterize the world are closely related to various omissions and commissions that need to be overcome, particularly in institutional arrangements. Global policies have a role here (for example, in defending democracy, and supporting schooling and international health facilities), but there is a need also to re-examine the adequacy of global institutional arrangements. The distribution of the benefits in the global economy depends, among other things, on a variety of global institutional arrangements, including trade agreements, medical initiatives, educational exchanges, facilities for technological dissemination, ecological and environmental restraints, and fair treatment of accumulated debts, often incurred by irresponsible military rulers of the past.

In addition to the momentous *omissions* that need to be rectified, there are also serious problems of *commission* that must be addressed for even elementary global justice. These include not only inefficient as well as inequitable trade restrictions that repress exports from the poorer countries, but also patent laws which can serve as counterproductive barriers to the use of life-saving drugs—vital for diseases like AIDS—and can provide inadequate incentive for medical research aimed at developing non-repeating medicine, such as vaccines.

Another global 'commission' that causes intense misery as well as lasting deprivation relates to the involvement of the world powers in the globalized trade in arms. This is a field in which a new global initiative is urgently required, going beyond the need—the very important need—to curb terrorism, on which the focus is so heavily concentrated right now. Local wars and military conflicts, which have very destructive consequences (not least on the economic prospects of poor countries), draw not only on regional tensions, but also on the global trade in arms and weapons. The world economic establishment is firmly entrenched in this business: the G-8 countries have been responsible for more than four-fifths of the international export of arms and armaments for many years. The United States alone is responsible for about half the world export of arms to other countries—nearly two-thirds of it to the developing countries. Indeed, the world leaders who express deep frustration at the irresponsibility of anti-globalization protesters lead the countries that make the most money in this terrible trade.

If there is some difficulty in seeing that justice is being done in the global world, this is not just an optical illusion. The task of global justice is a shared responsibility. It is a constructive exercise that calls for political and social reforms as well as economic engagement. The market mechanism is as good as the company it keeps.

Notes and References

1. This is discussed more fully in *Development as Freedom* (New York: Knopf, 1999).

2. J.F. Nash, 'The Bargaining Problem', *Econometrica*, volume 18 (1950).

THE COUNTRY OF FIRST BOYS

First appeared in *The Little Magazine: Education and Catastrophe,* volume VI, issues 1 and 2 (2005), pp. 7–17.

"I love to lose myself in a mystery," said Thomas Browne, the distinguished English physician in his book *Religio Medici*, published in 1643. While I would probably refrain from seeking out a doctor who has that particular preference (or for that matter, one who writes a book called *Religio Medici*), I would, however, happily convey some good news to him. The state of Indian education today, I could tell Thomas Browne, can offer him exactly the object of his love—the opportunity of thoroughly losing himself in a genuine and distinctive mystery.

How so? Those who have looked into the state of Indian education at all seriously know how poor, how deficient it is in coverage and quality. And yet Indian education receives spectacular acclaim from abroad. We are told that well-trained Indian experts are taking away good jobs from previously unthreatened Westerners. Leading American papers have carried articles urging improvements of the education and training for Americans, in order to keep up with that learned lot from distant Asia who are as accomplished as they are pushy. As I write this, I can see on the TV in my hotel in Italy the outpourings of a cable channel preoccupied with describing the 90 or so countries to which India sends its education-oriented products. From India? With a third of its people who can't even read or write? There is surely a *huge* mystery in all this.

It is, of course, hard to avoid the suspicion that American and European worries reflect nothing other than good, old-fashioned paranoia. But that way of squaring the circle would be hard to nurture given the actual presence of Indians in leading positions in Western academia, management, administration, literature, medical practice, engineering, and scientific and technological research. They are certainly a well-educated lot—no doubt about that. Aside from those who have been mainly educated in India (and evidently radiate the glory of Indian training and edification), the others who finished their education abroad had, we are told, such good grounding in their earlier instruction in India, that they could jump immediately to top performance as they hit Western educational establishments. There is a story of some splendour here.

Preoccupations and Priorities

But how easily does this resplendent picture sit with the huge mess that is Indian education? The answer, I am afraid, is that it sits there very comfortably, and what is worse, sits snugly in a very stable way. At every level, Indian education is obsessed with the first boys. In the classroom, in society and in the making of public policy.

In each class, the teachers revel in the success of the first boys, and many of these young wonders recollect throughout their lives that they were first boys—no less—in their class. I remember being really struck many years ago when one of the great men India has produced, who was then the Union Minister for Education and would later become the Prime Minister, could still remember—and was able to tell me—the marks he had received in school and college. Even though, I should explain, his marks were excellent (if I am any judge), I was impressed by what could only be described as his immense modesty in remaining so captivated by his student-day grades (similar to those of other brilliant students across the land), even after he had left nearly every Indian behind in the political life of India (aside from being—I am afraid I am giving away too many clues here—a talented novelist). No, the 'first boy syndrome' is certainly big in our country, and afflicts even persons of truly exceptional achievement outside the classroom.

For individuals this may, in fact, be no more than an amiable peculiarity which need not distract us from our admiration for the persons involved. But when the first boy syndrome takes over an educational system (as I fear has happened in India), there are reasons to be seriously alarmed. The priorities can get oddly distorted when the focus is so narrow, and the concentration of public policy is so strongly on looking after those blessed with opportunity and success. Not only do the educationally advantaged go, as we would expect, to schools, colleges, universities, and distinguished technological institutes (while hundreds of millions of Indian children do not manage to get primary education), but also the educational establishments they go to are, often enough, very fine (sometimes superb), in contrast with the low (sometimes dismal) quality of Indian schools and colleges in general.

We can find a nice chain of actions and reactions here. The system makes sure that some young people, out of a huge pool of the young, manage to get privileged education. The picking is done not through any organized attempt to keep anyone out (indeed, far from it), but through differentiations that are driven by economic and social inequality related to class, gender, location, and social privilege. The privileged, to their credit, by and large do very well—they don't waste opportunities. Their well-earned success comes, first, in the educational establishments themselves, and then in the world at large, impressing Indians and foreigners alike. The country then celebrates with abandon the 'nation's triumphs'. Furthermore, not only do the first boys do well in life, they can also relish— of course with becoming modesty—the homage they receive for having 'done their country proud'. Meanwhile, the last boys, and particularly the last girls, can't even read, not having had the opportunity of going to a decent school—or any school at all. But even they, when they learn about the great accomplishments of well-educated Indians, also celebrate their achievements and take pride in 'India's success'. So everyone, it appears, is happy, and no one jumps up and down in anger.

I should explain that I have nothing against the first boys. We certainly do need them for many different purposes: for academia to flourish, for businesses to prosper, for science and technology to move on, for medicine to progress, for people to feel self-reliant and capable, and, of course, for the cultivation of quality and high standards. My questions do not arise from any sense that the first boys are letting us down, or not doing what they might be expected to do. They are doing just fine for themselves and even for others, given the circumstances, and cannot be generally accused of rapacity or cupidity.

The question that has to be asked, however, is how unequal can the educational hierarchy be, without being not only terribly unjust to the people who are neglected and left out, but also extraordinarily inefficient when it is judged as a general social system. It is in that structural perspective, combining considerations of efficiency with equity, that we can best understand how—and how much—the country loses through its extraordinary concentration on first boys.

Aggregative Penalties of Disparity

Why should we, the question can be asked, particularly grumble about inequalities and gaps in Indian education when it is already achieving so much? Haven't you heard that the economy is moving nicely forward, and that our first boys are celebrated all over the world and even envied?

The most foundational issue is, of course, one of injustice. Not to be able to read or write or count or communicate is a tremendous deprivation and a great violation of the elementary freedoms that we all have reason to value and want. Serious issues of justice arise not only when a great many people are denied the opportunity of enjoying these centrally important freedoms, but also—going on from there—when the facilities to develop our basic capabilities are so unequally distributed by the society and the State. I shall try to say a bit more on this presently, but let me consider, before that, the aggregative—allegedly 'social'—perspectives that are often invoked ('fine economy', 'well-trained people', 'India twinkling', even if we must—hush, hush—avoid the polluted word 'shining'). They serve to keep our eyes firmly shut on what are dismissively called 'individual concerns'. Aren't we meant to be socially oriented? How can we miss the big picture of the nation's success, and whine about some who are left behind?

So, what does the aggregate picture look like? The Indian economy may be doing much better than before in many different ways, and yet it is still paying quite a heavy price for having a far less educated general labour force (as opposed to holders of special skills and recipients of technical training) than, say, China. For example, the commodity pattern of Indian exports is still very dependent on traditional products that need very little education to make, in addition to what can be well produced with the help of specialized skills of the privileged Indians (such as information products, electronic software, or call centre services that draw on fluency in English and the affability of style that the Indian middle classes can easily master). India has great difficulty in competing in a whole range of simple products the making of which requires basic education (and an ability to follow written instructions, but not much more), including elementary gadgets such as clocks and calculators and even computer hardware (no great mathematical skill needed there), in which China excels, and which were among the mainstays of the earlier 'East Asian Miracle'.

I have discussed elsewhere, along with Jean Drèze, the China–India contrasts, as well as those with other high economic performers, such as South Korea, Taiwan, Thailand, and other dynamic economies.[1] The lack of general education is still, alas, an important economic constraint, and will be more and more strongly felt as the size of Indian exports expand and we need to go beyond relying on traditional merchandise and the narrow range of products fashioned out of the highly trained skills of a limited group of people.

It is also worth noting that even the extent of the success of higher or specialized education must be dependent on the expanse and previous training of what we may call the 'catch-ment population' from which it draws its recruits. Given the number of people who receive no school education, and the number who get really below-par instruction at school, the quality of entry into higher or specialized education is severely reduced, and this cuts into the effectiveness of these 'later' educational activities. Our first boys may have to work quite a bit harder, if they were to retain their comparative position, once those disqualified by class or gender or location or social position can enter effectively to compete with the present-day champions. The enormous waste of massive talents resulting from bad—or no—school education cannot but be relevant even for the aggregative picture.

Even without raising the central issue of social justice, there are, thus, significant aggregative and efficiency considerations in assessing what India loses through its educational disparities, particularly from the inadequate coverage and frequently defi-cient quality of school education. However, questions of justice are very central in assessing the asymmetries and inequalities in Indian education, and this is where the unacceptability of the present situation becomes utterly and manifestly clear.

Unfreedom and Many-sided Deprivations

Lack of educational opportunities afflicts the lives and free-doms of a large proportion of Indians. At the time of the last census in 2001, a quarter of Indian men, and about half of the Indian women, were illiterate.[2] The proportions of Indian people condemned to live without letters and numbers are not only much larger than the corresponding ratios in China, South Korea, or Vietnam, but also substantially larger than the average of all the poor countries taken together (even after excluding China from that list), including substantial parts of Africa.[3] Further, the picture of educational deficiency is depressing not only in terms of the ratio of illiterates in the total population, but also judged by the proportion of children of school-going age who still miss the opportunity of going to school. While the statistics of the Ministry of Education systematically over-report school attendance (there are inherent biases in counting heads and determining financial allocations), it is clear from other sources of information, including National Sample Surveys and National Family Health Surveys, that—even though attendance has definitely increased over recent years—we are still nowhere near universal coverage.[4]

That a great many citizens should be doomed to such basic unfreedom is certainly a matter of political concern and must be of great relevance in the assessment of social justice. Furthermore, not only is this violation of significance of its own, it also leads to other deprivations which too are matters of considerable social gravity. Let me briefly mention a few of these concerns.

First, basic education can be very important in helping people to get jobs and gainful employment. This connection, while always present, is particularly critical in a rapidly globalizing world in which quality control and production according to strict specification can be quite crucial. The stellar performance of the first boys does not eliminate this vital need, since education influences the job opportunities of all and is crucial for the removal of economic poverty.

Second, when people are illiterate, their ability to understand and invoke their legal rights can be very limited. This can, for example, be a significant barrier for illiterate women to make use even of the rather limited legal rights that they do actually have.[5] Lack of schooling can directly lead to insecurities by distancing the deprived from the ways and means of resisting the violation of established rights.

Third, illiteracy can also muffle the political voice of the underdog and thus contribute directly to their insecurity. The connection between voice and security is often underestimated. This is not to deny that democracies can be effective even when many people are still illiterate: this point certainly needs emphasizing because it is missed in the deeply reactionary argument, which is often aired, that an illiterate population has no use for democratic rights. It is nevertheless the case that the reach of people's democratic voice can be much greater when political opportunities are combined with social empowerment, including the ability to read newspapers, periodicals, and books, and to communicate with each other. The issue is not whether democracies can be at all effective, but how much more effective they can become if the voices of people muffled by illiteracy can be liberated from the smothering that the state of Indian school education produces.

Fourth, basic education can play a major role in tackling health problems in general and epidemics in particular. It is easy to see the importance of specialized health education (for example, about the ways in which infections spread and how diseases can be prevented). But even general education can broaden a person's lines of thinking and generate social understanding in ways that may be extremely important in facing epidemiological problems. Indeed, many studies have suggested that general school education has a bigger impact on health than specialized health education itself has.[6]

Fifth, there is now extensive evidence that the schooling of young women can substantially enhance the voice and power of women in family decisions. Aside from the general importance of equity within the family, the voice of women can also lead to many other social changes. For example, women's empowerment tends to have a strong downward impact on the fertility rate. There is, in fact, considerable empirical evidence that fertility rates go down sharply with women's literacy and education (and also with women's income earning capacities) mainly because of their favourable effects on the empowerment of women. This is not surprising, since the lives that are most battered by the frequent bearing and rearing of children are those of young women, and anything that enhances their decisional power and increases the attention that their interests receive tend, in general, to prevent over-frequent child bearing. For example, in a comparative study of the different districts within India, it emerges that women's education and women's gainful employment are the two most important influences in reducing fertility rates.[7]

There is also much evidence that women's education and literacy tend to reduce the mortality rates of children. This is consistent with growing evidence of a close relationship between female literacy and child survival in many other countries as well.[8]

So the neglect of basic education of a large section of the Indian population causes many economic, social, and political adversities.[9] It compromises the basic freedoms of the neglected people, violating what can be seen as their human rights. It also reduces employment opportunities, legal protections, political voice, family health, reproductive freedom, and the social influence that the people left out can have. And going beyond that, even the interests of children can be badly affected. All this is in addition to the directly aggregative adversities that result from the reduction of economic potential because of a badly educated general labour force, and also from compromised educational advancements even at the peak because of restricted entry into the catchment population for higher and specialized education.

Barriers and Policy Priorities

The difference that basic education can make to human life is easy to see. It is also readily appreciated even by the poorest of families. Speaking personally, it has been wonderful for me to observe how easily the importance of education is perceived even by the poorest and the most deprived of families in India. This emerges *inter alia* from some studies on primary education in India that we have been undertaking (through the Pratichi Trust—a trust aimed at basic education, basic health care, and gender equity that was set up in India and Bangladesh using the Nobel Prize money I was lucky to get in 1998).[10] As the results of these studies have gradually come in, it has been remarkable to see how parents from the poorest and most depressed families long to give good education to their children (girls as well as boys), so that they grow up without the terrible handicaps from which the parents had themselves suffered. A similar general finding had powerfully emerged also from the much larger study on basic education in India that was undertaken by the PROBE team, published in 1999.[11]

Indeed, contrary to claims often made, we have not observed any basic reluctance by parents to send their children—daughters as well as sons—to school, provided affordable, effective, and safe schooling opportunities actually exist in their neighbourhood. Of course, there are many obstacles in giving shape to the dreams of parents. The economic circumstances of the families often make it very hard for them to send their children to school, particularly when there are fees or other charges to be paid. In the Pratichi Trust's latest study—that of primary education in the city of Calcutta—this has emerged as a discouraging factor in those publicly funded schools in which some payments are demanded (though we have been assured by those involved in educational planning in the Government of West Bengal that this problem will be eliminated as the delivery of primary education in Calcutta is comprehensively re-examined and restructured). Free elementary education is the right of all Indian children, and ways and means for making that a reality have to be found and guaranteed.

I am, of course, aware that some champions of unfettered use of the free market want to leave school fees to market forces, and are thrilled by the speedy expansion of private schools in India. This can hardly be the solution, though, given the limited incomes and resources of so many families, and also, if we take economic theory seriously (as I fear I do), given the asymmetry of information (in this case between the providers and consumers of school education) on which so much has been written in professional economics in recent years. But the basic issue is the need to recognize the fundamental entitlement and human right of everyone to decent facilities for schooling. Indeed, Adam Smith, who provided the classic analysis of the power and reach of the market mechanism two and a quarter centuries ago (and whom the market fundamentalists like quoting on *other* subjects), wrote eloquently on why it would be quite wrong to entrust schooling to the market: "For a very small expense the publik can facilitate, can encourage, and can even impose upon almost the whole body of the people, the necessity of acquiring those most essential parts of education."[12]

In fact, as Adam Smith expected, all the cases of speedy use of the opportunities of global commerce, with profound effects on the removal of poverty and economic deprivation, have drawn on the use of basic education for all citizens. For example, in Japan, the task was seen with remarkable clarity already in the mid-nineteenth century. The Fundamental Code of Education, issued in 1872 (shortly after the Meiji Restoration in 1868), expressed the public commitment to make sure that there must be 'no community with an illiterate family, nor a family with an illiterate person.'

Thus began—with the closing of educational gaps—Japan's remarkable history of rapid economic development. By 1910, Japan was almost fully literate; India is still far behind that a hundred years later. Incidentally, by 1913 Japan, though still much poorer than Britain or America, was publishing more books than Britain and more than twice as many as the United States. The concentration on education determined, to a large extent, the nature and speed of Japan's economic and social progress.

Later on, particularly in the second half of the twentieth century, South Korea, China, Taiwan, Hong Kong, Singapore,

Thailand, and other economies in East and Southeast Asia followed similar routes, partly inspired by the Japanese experience. They focused firmly on the general and comprehensive expansion of school education. Those economists and policy advisors who talk a great deal—righly—about what India can learn from these economies, particularly in the way they have made excellent use of the opportunities of economic globalization, should go on to compare the financial commitments of public money that each of these countries—without exception—made, compared with the relatively moderate sums that India has chosen to devote to this task (even though the recent enhancement of funding for school education by the government is a constructive and much overdue move in the right direction).

Funding, however, is not the only problem that basic education faces in India. There are other obstacles, too. A major difficulty lies in the weak institutional structure of primary schools in most areas of India. Extensive inefficiencies in operation are reinforced by particular inequities in the failure to provide fair opportunity to children from less privileged backgrounds. The difficulties are especially severe in bringing first generation school attenders into a caring and sympathetic system of primary instruction. There are too many complex issues here to make it easy to provide a quick summary of some of the policy problems that have been identified in the studies undertaken by the Pratichi Trust. But it is perhaps still useful to mention just a few of them that have not received the attention they deserve.

One problem arises from considerable irregularity in attendance by teachers in primary schools, which is understandably a subject of great parental dissatisfaction. While primary school teachers are no longer underpaid like they used to be

(I remember going out in demonstrations in Calcutta in my college days in support of their demand for what would seem very modest now), any hope that their large salary increases in recent years would lead to the elimination of teacher absenteeism and of the neglect of pupils from poor and socially disadvantaged families has not been realized.

In fact, in several cases we found, in the Pratichi studies, evidence of a new class division that put the well remunerated teachers at a big social and psychological distance from the children from poor, landless families, who are among the most neglected kids in schools. To remedy this, we need cooperation from the teachers' unions. We have, in fact, received very encouraging responses from some of the unions with which the Pratichi Trust has been in touch in West Bengal, even though there is, obviously, still a long way to go to translate this genuine resolve into effective implementation.

Second, related to this issue, there is also evidence of a fairly extensive breakdown of the system of school inspection. In some of the areas we studied, none of the schools had been inspected at all in the previous year. In conversations we had, the inspectors also expressed some helplessness in not being able to be frank about what they would like to report, given the power structure involved, particularly of rural administration. The recognition that a well-functioning system of inspection is a basic necessity for quality control in a profession where jobs are entirely secure has to be reflected in the reform of the institutional structure of primary education.

Third, one of the most important issues to address is the need to increase the voice of parents in the running of schools. The parent–teacher committees have often been extremely ineffective, and sometimes comprehensively non-functioning. Since the early reports of the Pratichi Trust on primary education in West Bengal, we have been happy to see the introduction of 'mother–teacher' committees in many parts of rural West Bengal (though none yet in Calcutta), and wherever they have been properly set up, they seem to have been very effective.

Fourth, the extraordinary dependence on private tuition of primary school children (for those who can afford to pay the tuition fees) reflects the low quality of what happens in the schools. But they also bring out in sharp focus the problems of economic inequality which allow the escape of some (those who can afford it) from unreliable dependence on primary schools, compared with others who cannot afford it at all (or are ruined through spending a high proportion of their meagre incomes in trying to do the best for their children). The escape route also makes the parents from more affluent—and typically more influential—families take far less interest in improving the quality of what happens in the schools themselves. The underlying problems cannot be solved just by banning the system of private tuition, and what must be addressed are the inefficiencies and neglects that have become standard parts of the school system in many areas of India.

Fifth, despite central support for cooked mid-day meals, the system is not yet in operation in many parts of the country. Since Indian children suffer not only from educational neglect but also from undernourishment on a scale that makes India a world-beater in an unenviable role, the effectiveness of mid-day meals can be very large indeed, in jointly addressing several pivotal problems together. Our observation is that in areas where the system has been recently introduced, it has been extremely popular, has raised the attendance of children, and has made a contribution to their health and happiness. It has also done something to make the absenteeism of teachers less pronounced. Perhaps this is not surprising, since it is one thing not to come to teach, which would affect the future of children in the long run, but quite another not to show up to unlock the stores where food and preparatory materials are kept for the cooking to proceed, which would lead to an intense clamour from disappointed children right here and now.

Again, India's social divisions are quite strongly felt here, as they are with the differential use of private tuition. There has been much protest from the parents in richer families about the quality of the food that is served, which has sometimes been justified, but at other times mainly reflected the differences in what the richer and poorer students can respectively afford. This is not quite the division between the 'first boys' and the rest, but it is part of the divisiveness of economic and social stratification in India. Interestingly enough, the dissatisfaction of the rich parents with the quality of food has received rather greater attention in the media than the happiness of better-fed kids from the poorer families has managed to attract. The media has a big role in drawing attention more effectively to the terrible—but entirely remediable—problems that blight the lives and future of the neglected school-age children of India.

The Syntax of Social Change

There are a great many changes in institutional arrangements and social facilities, in administrative provisions and union cooperation, that are urgently needed right now to bring decent basic education within the reach of all children in India. Money is not the only problem. And yet, financial commitment is also important, particularly in a country which stands out for its robust history of neglecting universal public education, in a way that Japan or China or Korea or Thailand or Vietnam, with their diverse political systems, definitely do not.

For a country so obsessed with the first boys—and increasingly with first girls too—there is, of course, the consolation meanwhile that they are doing just fine. There is indeed nothing to be ashamed of in celebrating the skill with which Greeshma Salin, a 22-year-old teacher in Cochin, educates Daniela Marinaro, a child of 13 in Malibu, California, on English grammar, over the Internet. She is evidently doing a great job, as *The New York Times* reports.[13] She is right, for example, to react to 'Daniela thinks that Daniela should give Daniela's horse Scarlett to Daniela's sister,' with the splendid pedagogic response, "Is this an awkward sentence? How can you make it better?"

Some day, I hope, Greeshma will have the opportunity to help to make a better sentence out of: 'India thinks that India should devote more of India's economic resources, organizational capacity, and social commitment to India's neglected children.' The syntax of that awkward sentence would definitely need fixing. But the country of first boys would need fixing first.

Notes and References

1. Jean Drèze and Amartya Sen, *India: Development and Participation* (Delhi and Oxford: Oxford University Press, 2002).

2. See Table 2.8 and related presentations in National Council of Educational Research and Training, *Compendium of Educational Statistics (School Education)* (New Delhi, 2002).

3. For comparative numbers, see Drèze and Sen, *India: Development and Participation* (2002), chapters 1–5 and the Statistical Appendix.

4. In Drèze and Sen, *India: Development and Participation* (2002), we have discussed the variety of information on this subject, including a relatively recent National Sample Survey (1995–6) and National Health Survey (1998–9).

5. See, for example, Salma Sobhan, *Legal Status of Women in Bangladesh* (Dhaka: Bangladesh Institute of Legal and International Affairs, 1978).

6. The connection between education and health is one of the subjects being investigated in the Global Equity Center at Harvard University led by Lincoln Chen.

7. See Mamta Murthi, Anne-Catherine Guio, and Jean Drèze, 'Mortality, Fertility and Gender Bias in India', *Population and Development Review*, volume 26 (December 1995), and the follow-up essay by Drèze and Murthi, 'Fertility, Education and Development: Evidence from India', *Population and Development Review*, volume 27 (2001).

8. See, among other important contributions, J.C. Caldwell, 'Routes to Low Mortality in Poor Countries', *Population and Development Review*, volume 12 (1986) and J.R. Behrman and B.L. Wolfe, 'How Does Mother's Schooling Affect Family Health, Nutrition, Medical Care Usage and Household Sanitation', *Journal of Econometrics*, volume 36 (1987).

9. These interdependences, which work through interlinked human agency, are discussed in my *Development as Freedom* (New York: Knopf; and Delhi and Oxford: Oxford University Press, 1999).

10. For examples, see *The Pratichi Education Report*, volume I (Delhi: TLM Books, 2002).

11. *Public Report on Basic Education in India* (New Delhi: Oxford University Press, 1999).

12. Adam Smith, *An Inquiry into the Nature and Causes of the Wealth of Nations* (1776), republished in R.H. Campbell and A.S. Skinner (eds), (Oxford: Clarendon Press, 1976), I.ii (p. 27) and V.i.f. (p. 785).

13. 'Latest in Outsourcing: Homework', reprinted in the *International Herald Tribune*, 8 September 2005.

POVERTY, WAR AND PEACE

This essay is the text of the Nadine Gordimer Lecture delivered at Witwatersrand University, Johannesburg, and University of Cape Town, South Africa, April 2007.

First appeared in *The Little Magazine: Security*, volume VII, issues 3 and 4 (2008), pp. 6–16.

The question of violence engaged Nadine Gordimer and Kenzaburō Ōe in a correspondence the two great writers had in 1998.[1] Gordimer noted that she "should not have been surprised" that in writing to each other they were so "preoccupied by the question of violence." She went on to explain: "This is a 'recognition' between two writers, but it goes further. It is the recognition of writers' inescapable need to read the signs society gives out cryptically and to try to make sense of what these really mean." That need—indeed, the inescapable need—to understand the question of violence not only influences writers like Gordimer and Ōe who illuminate us with their perceptive insights, but also makes all of us worry and fret and wonder in trying to understand what we ourselves observe and what we can learn from reading others, and what we could possibly add of our own, if we only knew how.

The signs that "society gives out cryptically", to use Gordimer's discerning phrase, engage us all in one way or another. Questions of violence and insecurity are omnipresent in the world around us. If peace is in our dreams, war and violence are constantly in our eyes and ears, and their terrible role in generating human insecurity is recognized across the world.[2]

The world of social science, to which I largely belong, has been trying hard to follow up our simple concerns with empirical studies. I do not, however, think we have got very far in our understanding. Indeed, the pursuit of questions of human security and its violation has been, to some extent, hampered by the priority given to other questions, often of a more aggregative kind, such as the economic growth of countries and regions, overall social and economic development of different parts of the world, and the demands of national security. The good news, however, is that the subject of human security is receiving greater attention in social studies than it had until rather recently, and certainly human security has become something of a new field of systematic research. There are investigations of the nature, content, and demands of human security, and of the ways and means of reducing, and when possible removing, the insecurities that plague human lives.

The idea of human security contrasts with the notion of 'national security' or 'state security', which concentrates primarily on safeguarding what is perceived as national robustness, which has only an indirect connection with the security of human beings who live in these states. National security, in that aggregative and somewhat distanced form, has been studied over the centuries, and it is fortunate for us—people living in different countries in the world—that the demands of human security, which can go well beyond the concerns of national security, are receiving more global attention today. Examination of the sources of insecurity of human lives, coming from violence, poverty, disease, and other widespread maladies, brings to light the far-reaching role of social, economic, political, and cultural influences that the limited concept of national security cannot capture.

That contrast may be clear enough, but in delineating human security adequately, it is also important to understand how the idea of human security relates to—and differs from—other human centred concepts, such as human development. These concepts, and perhaps most notably the important concept of human development, are not alienated from individual human lives in the way the pursuit of national security often tends to be, but they too have their own specialized priorities, which need not be the same as the concerns of human security. It is, therefore, particularly important to ask what the idea of human security adds to these well-established ideas, particularly human development.

The human development approach, pioneered among others by the visionary economist Mahbub ul Haq, has done much to enrich and broaden the literature on development. In particular, it has helped to shift the focus of developmental attention away from an overarching concentration on the growth of inanimate objects of convenience, such as commodities produced (reflected in the gross domestic product or the gross national product), to the quality and richness of human lives, which depend on a great many influences, of which commodity production is only one. Human development is concerned with removing the various hindrances that restrain and restrict human lives, and prevent its blossoming. Some of these concerns are captured in the much-used 'human development index' (HDI), which has served as something of a flagship of the human development approach, but the human development approach as a whole is much broader than what can be encapsulated into one numerical index of HDI. The wide range and long reach of the human development perspective have motivated a vast literature, with increasing informational coverage of different aspects of human lives.[3]

The idea of human development does, however, have a specially buoyant quality, since it is concerned with progress and augmentation. It is, as it were, out to conquer fresh territory on behalf of enhancing human lives, and for that reason perhaps far too upbeat to focus on rearguard actions needed to secure what has to be safeguarded. This is where the notion of human security becomes particularly relevant. Human security as an idea provides a necessary supplement to the expansionist perspective of human development for it pays direct attention to what in the insurance literature is called 'downside risks'. The insecurities that threaten human survival or the safety of daily life, or expose human beings to the uncertainty of disease and pestilence, or subject vulnerable people to abrupt penury related to economic downturns, or imperil the natural dignity of men and women, demand that special attention be paid to the dangers of sudden deprivation. Human security demands protection from these dangers and also calls for the empowerment of people so that they can cope with and overcome, and when possible prevent, the incidence and reach of these hazards.

I must, however, emphasize that there is no basic contradiction between the focus of human security and the subject matter of the human development approach. Indeed, from a quantitative perspective, protection and safeguarding can also be seen as augmentations of a sort, to wit, that of safety and security. But the emphasis and priorities are quite different in the cautious and individually articulated perspective of human security from what is typically found in the relatively sanguine and upward-focused literature on human development. Perhaps a less confrontational way of thinking of the connection is to argue for a broadening of the human development perspective to include concerns about the insecurities of human lives in addition to expanding positively what we are capable of doing with our lives.

⌘

Society does indeed give out cryptic signs, as Nadine Gordimer points out, of the causes of violence, and indeed of human insecurities of other kinds. I shall be concerned in this essay mainly with the insecurity linked to violence, but its connection with other sources of insecurity cannot be ignored in understanding the prevalence and impact of violence. On the grand subject of the root causes of contemporary global violence, theories abound—as theories are prone to. However, two particular lines of theorizing have come to receive much more attention than most others. One approach is primarily cultural and social, and often focuses on such concepts as identity, tradition, and civilization, and the other is largely economic and political, and tends to focus on poverty, inequality, and deprivation.

The main thesis I would like to present here is that the economic, social, and cultural issues need serious efforts at integration, an exercise that is spurned both by the crudely fatalistic theorists of civilizational clash and by the simple constructionist theorists who fall for the temptation to oversimplify the world which they wish to reform. I would argue, among other claims, that it is a mistake to look for ready-made reasons for remedying economic injustice that would appeal even to those who are, for whatever reason, not revolted by injustice itself and yet hate—or are terrified of—the threat of violence. I hope

I would be forgiven for the lack of elegance in giving away my main thesis towards the beginning of my essay. I fear I have never been particularly good in generating suspense, and I expect you would not be surprised to hear that no publisher has ever asked me to try my hand at writing a detective story.

Cultural theories tend to look at conflicts connected with modes of living as well as religious beliefs and social customs. That line of reasoning can lead to many different theories, some more sophisticated than others. It is perhaps remarkable that the particular cultural theory that has become the most popular in the world today is also perhaps the crudest. This is the approach of seeing global violence as the result of something that is called 'the clash of civilizations'. The approach defines some postulated entities that are called 'civilizations' in primarily religious terms, and it goes on to contrast the 'Islamic world', the 'Judeo-Christian Western world', the 'Buddhist world', the 'Hindu world', and so on. It is the intrinsic hostility among civilizations that make them prone, it is argued in this high theory, to clash with each other.[4]

Underlying the approach of civilizational clash is an oddly artificial view of history, according to which these distinct civilizations have grown separately, like trees on different plots of land, with very little overlap and interaction. And today, as these disparate civilizations with their divergent histories face one another in the global world, they are firmly inclined, we are told, to clash with each other—a tale, indeed a gripping tale, of what can, I suppose, be called hate at first sight. This make-believe account has little use for the long history of interactions and constructive movements of ideas and influences across the borders of countries and regions in so many different fields—literature, arts, music, mathematics, science, engineering, trade, commerce, and other human engagements. The civilizational theorists are not entirely wrong in assuming that people are often suspicious of foreigners about whom they know little—possibly only about a few odd beliefs and practices that 'those foreigners' are supposed to have—but more knowledge of each other can generate understanding rather than greater hostility. The civilizational theorists in this mode have tended to feed ignorant suspicion of 'the others' through their confident presumption that coming closer to each other as human beings must somehow aggravate those suspicions rather than helping to allay them.

Aside from missing out much of world history, the civilizational approach also takes a mind-boggling shortcut in trying to understand our sense of identity, with all its diversities and complexities, in terms of just a single sense of belonging, to wit, our alleged perception of oneness respectively with our so-called civilization. It is through this huge oversimplification that the job of understanding diverse human beings of the world is metamorphosed, in this rugged approach to humanity, into looking at the different civilizations: personal differences are then seen as if they must be parasitic on civilizational contrasts. Violence between persons is then interpreted, in this approximate theory, as animosity between distinct civilizations, which is a kind of all-powerful generic backdrop behind the frontage of human relations. Thus, in addition to its dependence on an imaginary history of the world, the civilizational explanation of global violence is firmly moored on a particular 'solitarist' approach to human identity, which sees human beings as members of exactly one group defined by their native civilization or religion.

A solitarist approach is, in fact, an excellent way of misunderstanding nearly everyone in the world. In our normal lives, we see ourselves as members of a variety of groups—we belong to all of them. The same person can be, without any contradiction, a South African citizen, of Asian origin, with Indian ancestry, a Christian, a socialist, a woman, a vegetarian, a jazz musician, a doctor, a feminist, a heterosexual, a believer in gay and lesbian rights, a jazz enthusiast, and one who believes that the most important problem that the world faces today is how to defeat Australia in world cricket. Each of these identities can be of significance to the person, depending on the problem at hand and the context of choice, and the priorities between them could be influenced by her own values as well as by social pressures. There is no reason to think that whatever civilizational identity a person has—religious, communal, regional, national, or global—must invariably dominate over every other relation or affiliation he or she may have.

Trying to understand global violence through the lens of the clash of civilizations does not bear much scrutiny because the reasoning is so crude, but it must also be recognized that reductionist cultivations of singular identities have indeed been responsible for a good deal of what can be called 'engineered bloodshed' across the world. But this results from the fomenting and cultivation of targeted differences, rather than being just a spontaneous outcome from a 'natural and inescapable' clash. We may be suddenly informed by instigators that we are not just Yugoslavs, but actually Serbs ('We absolutely don't like Albanians'), or that we are not just Rwandans or Kigalians or Africans, but specifically Hutus who must see Tutsis as enemies. I recollect from my own childhood in pre-Independent

India, how the Hindu-Muslim riots suddenly erupted in the 1940s, linked with the politics of Partition, and also the speed with which the broad human beings of summer were suddenly transformed, through ruthless cultivation of segregation, into brutal Hindus and fierce Muslims of the winter. Hundreds of thousands perished at the hands of people who, led by the designers of carnage, killed others on behalf of—for the cause of—those whom they abruptly identified as their 'own people'.

⤫⤫⤫

Identity politics can certainly be mobilized very effectively in the cause of violence.[5] And yet it can also be effectively resisted through a broader understanding of the richness of human identities. Our disparate associations may divide us in particular ways, and yet there are other identities, other affiliations, that defy any particular division. A Hutu who is recruited in the cause of chastising a Tutsi is also a Rwandan, and an African, possibly a Kigalian, and indubitably a human being—identities that the Tutsis also share. Socially and culturally anchored theories are not wrong in noting that people can be made to fight each other through incitement to violence across some divisive classification, but when that happens, we have to look for explanations of why and how the institutions occur, and how that one identity is made to look like the only one that matters. The process of such cultivated violence cannot really be seen simply as something like the unfolding of human destiny.[6]

In a marvellous essay in her book *Writing and Being*,[7] Nadine Gordimer quotes Proust's remark: "Do not be afraid to go too far, for the truth lies beyond." Gordimer is talking here about three great writers, Naguib Mahfouz, Chinua Achebe, and Amos Oz, respectively from Egypt, Nigeria, and Israel—countries that are not only very different in many ways, but which are also in some conflict with each other. Gordimar notes that "the oppositional links are there", and yet, she goes on to point out, "these three writers do not expound the obvious, divided by race, country and religion, they enter by their separate ways territory unknown, in a common pursuit that doesn't have to be acknowledged in any treaty."

The battle against the bloody illusion of destiny calls for clarity. A clearer understanding comes not only from the visions of insightful writers, but also in more mundane ways from the thoughts of very ordinary people. It is that understanding that the instigators want to break down, and here the powerful voice of the more insightful can give us all a determination that we may not find easy to sustain. When Mahatma Gandhi moved around, unarmed and completely unprotected, through the riot-torn districts during the violence of Indian Partition, he was not only bringing new ideas to some, but also helping to build greater determination of those whose own ideas matched, perhaps in a somewhat vague form, those of Gandhiji, but who did not have quite the courage and defiant confidence that Gandhi brought to them.

⋘☙⊙☙⋙

Aside from the need to disestablish the claim that alleged clashes of civilizations, religions, or communities must be natural processes, it is also important to appreciate that no matter how momentous the religious differences may appear to be in the context of some warfare today, there are other divisions that also have the potential for creating strife and carnage. The violence of solitarist identity can have a tremendously varying reach. Indeed, the obsession with religions and so-called civilizations (based primarily on religious differences) has been so strong in contemporary global politics that there is a strong tendency to forget how other lines of identity divisions have been exploited in the past—indeed not so long ago—to generate very different types of violence and war, causing millions of deaths.

For example, appeals to country and nationality played a rousing role in the immensely bloody war in Europe between 1914–18, and a shared religious background of Christianity did nothing to stop the Germans, the British, and the French from tearing each other apart. The identity that was championed then was that of nationalism, with the huge patriotic fervour it generated. Before the horrors of the First World War took the freshly recruited Wilfred Owen's life in the battlefield, he had the time to write his own protest about values that glorify violent combat in the cause of one's identity with one's nation and fatherland:

> My friend, you will not tell with such high zest
> To children ardent for some desperate glory,
> The old lie: *Dulce et Decorum est*
> *Pro Patria Mori.*

Horace's ringing endorsement of the honour of death for (or allegedly for) one's country could be seen as catering to the violence of nationalism, and it was this invocation against which Wilfred Owen was emphatically protesting.

Europeans today may not easily appreciate Owen's profound sense of frustration and protest. The understanding that seemed well 'beyond' the 'too far' in Europe during the First World War, or for that matter during the Second, is now altogether customary and commonplace across Europe. The Germans, the French, and the British mix with each other in peace and tranquility and sit together to decide what to do in their continent without reaching for their gun.

A similar vulnerability is present in many other divisions of identities that may, at one level, be made to look like an unstoppable march of violence based on its unique claim of importance, but which, at another—broader—level may be nothing other than an artificially fostered avowal that can be disputed and displaced by a great many other solidarities and loyalties associated with different identities, including—of course—the broad commonality of our shared humanity.

ↄ◖◗ↄ

Let me, for the moment, leave the cultural approaches there. What about the other approach, the one of political economy? This line of reasoning sees poverty and inequality as the root causes of violence. It is not hard to see that the injustice of inequality can generate intolerance and that the suffering of poverty can provoke anger and fury. There is clearly much plausibility in seeing a connection between violence and poverty. For example, many countries have experienced—and continue

to experience—the simultaneous presence of economic destitution and political strife. From Afghanistan and Sudan to
Somalia and Haiti, there are plenty of examples of the dual
adversities of deprivation and violence faced by people in different parts of the world. Given that coexistence, it is not at
all unnatural to ask whether poverty kills twice—first through
economic privation and second through political carnage.

Poverty can certainly make a person outraged and desperate,
and a sense of injustice can be a good ground for rebellion—
even bloody rebellion. Furthermore, it is not uncommon to
presume that a basic characteristic of an enlightened attitude
to war and peace must go beyond the obvious and immediate
causal features that can be plainly seen in a conflict and seek
'deeper' causes. In looking for such underlying causes, the economics of deprivation and inequity has a very plausible claim
to attention. The belief that the roots of discontent and disorder has to be sought in economic destitution has, thus, been
fairly widely favoured by social analysts trying to look beyond
the apparent and the obvious.

Also, the straightforward thesis linking poverty with violence
also has another appeal: that it looks ready for good use in the
humane advocacy of concerted public action to end poverty.
Those trying to eradicate poverty in the world are, naturally
enough, tempted to invoke the apparent causal connection
that ties violence to poverty, to seek the support of even those
who are not moved by poverty itself. There has, in fact, been an
increasing tendency in recent years to argue in favour of policies of poverty removal on the ground that this is the surest way
to prevent political strife and turmoil. Basing public policy—
international as well as domestic—on such an understanding

has some evident attractions. It provides a politically powerful argument for allocating more public resources and efforts on poverty removal because of its presumed political rewards, taking us much beyond the direct moral case for doing this.

Since widespread physical violence seems to be more loathed and feared, especially by well-placed people, than social inequity and the deprivation—even extreme deprivation—of others, it is indeed tempting to be able to tell all, including the well-heeled, that terrible poverty will generate terrifying violence. Given the visibility and public anxiety about wars and disorders, the indirect justification of poverty removal—not for its own sake but for pursuing peace and quiet—has become, in recent years, a dominant part of the rhetoric of fighting poverty.

There is certainly a connection there, but is it really plausible to seek explanations of violence in a one-factor analysis of poverty and privation? While the temptation to go in this direction is easy to appreciate, the difficulty here lies in the possibility that if the causal connection proves to be not quite robust, then economic reductionism would not only have impaired our understanding of the world, but would also tend to undermine the declared rationale of the public commitment to remove poverty. This is a particularly serious concern, since poverty and massive inequality are terrible enough in themselves to provide ample reason for working for their removal— even if they did not have any further ill effects through indirect links. Just as virtue is its own reward, poverty is at least its own punishment. To look for some ulterior reason for fighting poverty through its effects on violence and conflict may make the argument broader with a larger reach, but it can also make the reasoning much more fragile.

To see this danger is not the same as denying that poverty and inequality can—and do—have far-reaching connections with conflict and strife, but these connections have to be investigated and assessed with appropriate care and empirical strong-mindedness. The temptation to summon economic reductionism may be sometimes effective in helping what we may see as a right cause (and may even have the agreeable feature of catering to our frailty in giving us satisfaction from frightening the ethically obtuse by threatening bloody violence), but it is basically an unsound way to proceed and can indeed be seriously counterproductive for political ethics.

🙠🙡

The simple thesis linking poverty with violence is not only compromised by doubtful ethical use, it is also, as it happens, riddled with epistemic problems. The claim that poverty is responsible for group violence is empirically much too crude both because the linkage of poverty and violence is far from universally observed, and because there are other social factors that are also associated with poverty and violence.

When recently I gave the Lewis Mumford Lecture at the City College of New York, entitled 'The Urbanity of Calcutta', I had the opportunity to comment on the remarkable fact that Calcutta is not only one of the poorest cities in India—and indeed in the world—it so happens that it also has a very low crime rate. Indeed, in serious crimes, the poor city of Calcutta has the lowest incidence among all the Indian cities. The average incidence of murder in Indian cities (including all the 35 cities that are counted in that category) is 2.7 per 100,000 people—2.9 for Delhi. The rate is 0.3 in Calcutta.[8] The same lowness of violent crime can be seen in looking at the total number of all violations of the Indian Penal Code put together. It also applies to crime against women, the incidence of which is very substantially lower in Calcutta than in all other major cities in India.

It also emerges that while Calcutta is by a long margin the city with the lowest homicide rate in India, the Indian cities in general are strikingly low in the incidence of violent crime by world standards, and are beaten only by much richer and more well-placed cities like Hong Kong and Singapore. Here are some numbers relating to 2005, the closest year for which we could get data. Paris has a homicide rate of 2.3, London of 2.4, Dhaka of 3.6, New York of 5.0, Buenos Aires of 6.4, Los Angeles 8.8, Mexico City 17.0, Johannesburg 21.5, Sao Paulo 24.0, and Rio de Janeiro an astonishing 34.9.[9] In India, only Patna in the troubled state of Bihar is in the big league with a figure of 14.0 as the homicide rate—no other Indian city gets even to half that number, and the average of Indian cities is, as mentioned earlier, only 2.7. Even the famously low-crime Japanese cities have more than three times the murder rate of Calcutta, with 1.0 per 100,000 for Tokyo and 1.8 for Osaka, and only Hong Kong and Singapore come close to Calcutta (though still more than 60 per cent higher), at 0.5 per 100,000, compared with Calcutta's 0.3.

If all this appears to us to be an unfathomable conundrum, given Calcutta's poverty, that may be a reflection of the limitation of our thought rather than a paradox of nature. Calcutta does, of course, have a long distance to go to eradicate poverty and to put its material house in order. It is important to remember that the low crime rate does not make those nasty problems go away. And yet there is something important to note, and even to celebrate, in the recognition that poverty does not inescapably produce violence, independently of political movements as well as social and cultural interactions.

Explanation of crime is not an easy subject for empirical generalizations, and even though there have been some attempts recently to understanding the nature and incidence of crime in terms of the characteristics of the respective neighbourhoods, it is quite clear that there is still a long way to go for a fuller understanding of the picture.[10] In my Mumford Lecture, I have tried to argue that Calcutta has, among other causal factors, benefited from the fact that it has had a long history of being a thoroughly mixed city, where neighbourhoods have not had the feature of sharp ethnic separation that some cities have—in India as well as elsewhere. There are also many other social and cultural features that are undoubtedly relevant in understanding the relation between poverty and crime. For example, in trying to understand the high rate of violent crime in South Africa, it would be hard to overlook the connection between the high incidence of urban violent crime and the legacy of apartheid. The linkage involves not only the inheritance of racial confrontation, but also the terrible effects of separated neighbourhoods and families that were split up for the economic arrangements that went with apartheid policies. But it would not be easy to explain why the belated attempts to generate mixed communities have also had the immediate effect of fostering crime committed within the newly mixed neighbourhoods. Perhaps the legacy of a long history may be hard to wipe out.

I am afraid we do not know enough about the empirical relations to be confident of what the exact causal connections are, and I am acutely aware that there is need for humility here that social sciences invariably invite and frequently do not get. It does, however, seem fairly clear that the tendency to see a universal and immediate link between poverty and violence would be very hard to sustain. There is certainly a more complex picture that lies beyond the alleged straightforwardness of the poverty–violence relationship.

More specifically, if we look, in particular, at violence related to religion, ethnicity, and community (the direction to which we are dispatched by many cultural theorists), the role of conscious politics as a barrier also demands a fuller recognition. For example, the prevailing politics of Calcutta and of West Bengal, which is very substantially left of centre (West Bengal has the longest history in the world of elected communist government, based on free multiparty elections for 30 years now), has tended to concentrate on deprivation related to class—and more recently gender. That altered focus, which is very distinct from religion gender. That altered focus, which is very distinct from religion and religion-based community, has made it much harder to exploit religious differences for instigating riots against minorities, as has happened, with much brutality, in some Indian cities, for example Bombay and Ahmedabad. Calcutta did have plentifully its share of Hindu–Muslim riots related to Partition, which were rampant across the subcontinent. But since then, over more than four decades, there have been no such riots in this large city, unlike in many other urban conglomerates in India. Indeed, the whole sectarian agenda of cultivating communal divisiveness seems to have got substantially overturned by new political and social priorities that dominate the city.

And in this political development, the focus on economic poverty and inequality seems to have played, if anything, a constructive role in bringing out the ultimate triviality of religious differences in preventing social harmony. In the recognition of plural human identities, the increased concentration on class and other sources of economic disparity has made it very hard to excite communal passions and violence in Calcutta along the lines of a religious divide—a previously cultivated device that has increasingly looked strangely primitive and raw. The minorities, mainly Muslims and Sikhs, have had a sense of security in Calcutta that they have not been able to enjoy in Bombay or Ahmedabad or Delhi.

If identities related to left-wing politics and class have had the effect of vastly weakening violence based on religious divisions and community contrasts in the Indian part of Bengal, a similar constructive influence can be seen on the other side of the border, in Bangladesh, coming from the power of identities of language, literature, and music, which do not divide Muslims and Hindus into different—and exploitably hostile—camps. The more general point here is that an understanding of multiplicity of our identities can be a huge force in combating the instigation of violence based on a singular identity—particularly religious identity, which is the dominant form of cultivated singularity in our disturbed world today.

❧❧❧

The economic connections between poverty and violence are quite complex and can hardly be captured by the simplicity of economic reductionism. For example, the violent history of Afghanistan cannot be unrelated to poverty and indigence that the population has experienced, and yet to reduce the causation of violence there entirely to this singular economic observation would be to miss out the role of the Taliban and the politics of religious fundamentalism. It would also leave out the part played by the history of Western military support—and incitement—to strengthen religious extremists in Afghanistan against the Russians at a time when the Western leaders saw the Soviet Union to be something like a single-handed 'axis of evil'. And, at the same time, to dissociate the rise of fundamentalism and sectarian violence from all economic connections would also be a mistake. We must try to understand the different interconnections that work together, and often kill together. We need some investigative sophistication to understand what part is played by the economic components in the larger structure of an interactive social framework.

The empirical connections between poverty and violence are clearly contingent on many other circumstances. There is, of course, no dearth of evidence of conflicts and confrontations in economies with a good deal of poverty and much inequality. But, at the same time, there are also other economies with no less poverty or inequality that seem to stay deeply and inertly sunk just in economic hardship, without generating serious political turbulence. Poverty can coexist with peace and apparent tranquility, and the causal reasoning linking poverty to violence has gaps that need to be acknowledged. Impoverishment can, of course, yield provocation to defy established laws and rules, but it need not give people the initiative, courage, and actual ability to do anything particularly violent.

Indeed, destitution can be accompanied not only by economic debility, but also by political impotence. The emaciated victims of deprivation can be too frail and too dejected to fight and battle, and even to protest and holler. It is, thus, not surprising that often enough intense suffering and inequity have been accompanied by astonishing peace and deafening silence. For example, severe famines have, in fact, occurred without there being much rebellion or strife or warfare. For example, the famine years in the 1840s in Ireland were among the most peaceful, and there was little attempt by the hungry masses to intervene even as ship after ship sailed down the river Shannon laden with food, carrying it away from starving Ireland to well-fed England, by the pull of market forces (the English had more money to buy meat, poultry, butter, and food items than the blighted Irish had). As it happens, the Irish do not have an exceptional reputation for excessive docility, and yet the famine years were, by and large, years of law and order and peace. London not only got away with extreme misgovernance of Ireland, they did not even have to face, then, the violence of Irish mobs, who were busy looking to escape hunger, to be soon followed by seeking ways and means of emigrating out of the country. (Even though the Irish famines had the largest share of mortality in total population among all the famines for which data exist, almost the same proportion left the country, mostly for America, following the famine.) As Calgacus, the rebellious Scottish chief, said—as reconstructed by Tacitus—about Roman dominance of first century Britain: "They make a wilderness and they call it peace."

This does not, however, indicate that the poverty, starvation, and inequity of the Irish famines had no long-run effects on violence in Ireland. Indeed, the memory of injustice and neglect had the effect of severely alienating the Irish from Britain, and contributed greatly to the violence that characterized Anglo-Irish relations over more than a century and a half. Economic destitution may not lead to an immediate rebellion, but it would be wrong to presume from this that there is no connection between poverty and violence. There is an important need here to look at connections over time—often, a very long time—and also at the way the grievances of deprivation and maltreatment get merged with other factors, including, in the Irish case, a championing of national identity that seeks distancing from the English. The offensive nature of English caricatures of the Irish, going back all the way to Spenser's *Faerie Queene* in the sixteenth century, would be strongly reinforced by the experience of the famines of the 1840s under British rule, generating deep resentment against Ireland's more powerful neighbours who did so little to stop the starvation, and in many ways, even helped to aggravate it.

There is a similarity here with the experience of the Middle East. There are, of course, many influences that make the situation as terrible as it is there right now, including the apparent inability of the US administration to think clearly—not to mention humanely—on the subject. But among the many connections, it is hard to ignore the memory of ill-treatment of the Middle East by Western powers during the colonial days, when the new masters could subdue one nation after another and draw—and redraw—the boundaries between countries in that ancient land just as they wanted. That abuse of power did not cause many riots right then in the nineteenth century, but that silence of the vanquished—the peace of the trampled—does not indicate that the subject matter was gone forever, and would not leave behind a terrible memory of ill-treatment. As Flora Goforth remarked in Tennessee Williams's *The Milk Train Does Not Stop Here Anymore*, "Life is all memory except for the one present moment that goes by you so quick you hardly catch it going." Similarly, the new episodes of trampling and pulverization today—in Iraq and Palestine and elsewhere—will not be easily forgotten, I fear, for a long time in the future.

∾⊚⊙∾

If the strong but less immediate linking of poverty and injustice to violence has some plausibility (as I believe it does), then we have to see that ideas of identity and culture add to the reach of issues of political economy, rather than competing with their influence in an 'either this or that' way. The categories around which the provoked violence may proceed would have cultural and social distinctions of their own (linked with ethnicity or nationality or social background), but the possibility of instigating anger can be dramatically increased and magnified by historical association with economic and political inequity. Indeed, even the brutality of the Hutu activists against Tutsis made effective use of the fact that Tutsis had more of a privileged position in the Rwanda of earlier days than the Hutus typically had—this would have done nothing to justify what happened, but the existence of that empirical connection is part of the study of violence of which we have to take notice. Poverty and inequality must have a role in promoting and sustaining violence, but that role, I would argue, has to be sought not through an exclusive concentration on deprivation and destitution in isolation from society and culture, but through looking for a larger and much more extensive framework with interactive roles of poverty and other features of society.

Similarly, while the fierce nastiness of Al Qaeda against Western targets cannot be justified by any invoking of history, the fact that those in whose name the terrorists work have had unequal treatment in the past from Western colonialists makes the invitation to barbarity that much easier to sell. The absence of an ethnical justification of such a linkage does not eliminate the fact that it can nevertheless have much power in moving people to blind rage. Indeed, the tolerance of terrorism by an otherwise peaceful population is another peculiar phenomenon in many parts of the contemporary world, particularly those that feel they were badly treated in the past.

Inequalities of military strength, political power and economic might leave behind huge inheritances of discontent. This is so even when the process is not apparently linked with force and strong-arm behaviour, for example, the injustice of leaving hundreds of millions behind in global economic and social progress, or condemning millions of others to untreated medical maladies for ailments that can be eliminated or effectively controlled if the global economic mechanism did not fail to provide life-saving drugs to those who need them most.

∾○∿

The main thesis I have tried to present here is that the economic, social, and cultural issues need serious efforts at integration—an exercise that is spurned both by the fatalistic theorists of civilizational clash and by the hurried advocates of economic reductionism. Cultural and social factors as well as features of political economy are all quite important in understanding violence in the world today. But they do not work in isolation from each other, and we have to resist the tempting shortcuts that claim to deliver insight through their single-minded concentration on some one factor or another, ignoring other central features of an integrated picture. Perhaps most importantly, we have reason to understand that these distinct causal antecedents of violence are not immovable objects that can defy and overwhelm all human efforts to create a more tolerable social order.[11]

It is indeed important to see the often-neglected connection between clarity and reach of understanding and the way society functions and operates. Indeed, but for the political vision that inspired South Africa's anti-apartheid movement, led by Nelson Mandela, South Africa today would be characterized by violent revenge against what had been one of the crudest segregationist orders in the world. Similarly, but for the acceptance of what Gordimer calls the "common pursuit that doesn't have to be acknowledged in any treaty" (particularly under the leadership of Mahatma Gandhi), it would be hard to imagine a multireligious India that is so radically different today from the rioting days of the 1940s, and to expect that the political system of a country with more than 80 per cent Hindu population could sustain democratic politics of a kind that would result in India's having a Sikh Prime Minister and a Christian leader of the ruling party (and until recently, a Muslim President) to take the helm of Indian political affairs, without this appearing to be in any way out of place.

Similarly, the barbarity of world wars in the early twentieth century paved the way for the kind of social analyses that would ultimately lead to the submerging of those national conflicts within Europe in the latter half of the century in a way that would have been very hard to imagine in the trenches and battlefields in the dark days of 1914–18.

It is not remarkable that divisions can be exploited to generate violence, sometimes made more intense and fierce through the coupling of economic and social inequality with ethnic and cultural differences. Nor is it really surprising that those divisive lines of thinking can be overcome given some clarity of vision and understanding. What, however, is altogether magnificent is that what seems to lie beyond the 'too far' at one time may become thoroughly ordinary and entirely mundane at another. That recognition, which is important in general, may be especially so in our moments of dejection about human insecurity in the contemporary world.

Notes and References

1. Nadine Gordimer, *Living in Hope and History: Notes from the Century* (London: Bloomsbury, 1999), pp. 84–102.

2. A few years ago when, along with Dr Sadako Ogata, I was privileged to chair the Commission for Human Security which reported to Kofi Annan, the UN Secretary-General, and the Prime Minister of Japan (his government had taken the initiative in setting up this Commission), we were impressed to see how widely the interest in human security is shared across the world. Our report is called *Human Security Now* (UN Publications, 2003).

3. One source of such information is the annual series of Human Development Reports, published by the UN. However, the human

development perspective has influenced other sources of systematic information as well, for example, the World Bank's important annual publications in the form of the World Development Reports. The underlying rationale of the approach is discussed in *Development as Freedom* (New York: Knopf; and London and Delhi: Oxford University Press, 1999).

4. This theory has received its definitive exposition in Samuel Huntington's widely read book, *The Clash of Civilizations and the Remaking of World Order* (New York: Simon and Schuster, 1996).

5. An insightful assessment of the recent cultivation of communal strife in India, especially in Gujarat, can be found in Martha C. Nussbaum's *The Clash Within* (Delhi: Permanent Black, 2007).

6. This issue is examined in my book, *Identity and Violence: The Illusion of Destiny* (New York: W.W. Norton and Company, 2006; and London and Delhi: Penguin, 2007).

7. Nadine Gordimer, 'Zaabalawi: The Concealed Side', in *Writing and Being* (Cambridge, MA, USA: Harvard University Press, 1995), p. 43.

8. These figures are based on the data presented by the National Crime Record Bureau of India, *Crime in India 2005* (New Delhi: Government of India, 2007).

9. The crime rates of different cities have been collected from the respective municipal and national publications, and I am very grateful to Pedro Ramos Pinto for efficient research assistance in this and related work.

10. See, for example, the illuminating collection of essays in Per-Olof H. Wilkstrom and Robert J. Sampson (eds), *The Explanation of Crime: Context, Mechanisms and Development* (Cambridge, UK: Cambridge University Press, 2006).

11. These connections are more fully explored in the report of a Commonwealth Commission (*Civil Paths to Peace*, London: Marlborough House, 2007) which I was privileged to chair, with the assistance of a remarkable group of social and political thinkers drawn from right across the Commonwealth.

WHAT SHOULD KEEP US AWAKE
AT NIGHT

This is a slightly abridged and edited version of the inaugural Professor Hiren Mukerjee Memorial Annual Parliamentary Lecture, titled 'Demands of Social Justice', delivered in the Central Hall of Indian Parliament on 11 August 2008. Historian, writer, compelling orator, and Member of Parliament representing the Communist Party of India from 1952 to 1977, Professor Hirendranath Mukerjee was a liberal scholar who rejected ideological sectarianism in Indian politics.

First appeared in *The Little Magazine: Speak Up*, volume VIII, issues 1 and 2 (2009), pp. 8–15.

Hiren Mukerjee was something of a hero of mine for a very long time. Among his remarkable qualities and virtues, there were three things in particular that moved me greatly. The first was his overwhelming sympathy for and solidarity with the downtrodden people of India—indeed anywhere in the world. The hungry, the deprived, the jobless, the exploited, the insecure, always had the powerful voice of this political leader speaking up for them. The second was his overwhelming reliance on critical analysis and reasoning. The third characteristic that particularly appealed to me was Hiren Mukerjee's passion for Sanskrit and love of books in general. Perhaps I am biased since I strongly share those weaknesses. I remember being quite energized by Hiren Mukerjee's apt citations from Sanskrit classics in a great many of his parliamentary speeches, pointing out how ideas from old books can throw light on the new issues of the day. One had to run to the library or to a bookshop to follow up his insightful references.

I have chosen as my theme the prevalence and reach of inequity and injustice in India—what should really keep us awake at night. Despite India's rapid economic progress at the aggregate level, with booming markets for consumer goods—from cars to books—the country suffers still from great inequities. We have to go deeply into the nature of justice and injustice to appreciate the nature and durability of inequity and injustice in India.

In examining the demands of social justice in India, it is important to distinguish between an arrangement-focused view of justice, on the one hand, and a realization-focused under-standing of justice, on the other. Sometimes justice is concep-tualized in terms of certain organizational arrangements—some institutions, some regulations, some behavioural rules—the active presence of which indicates that justice is being done. The question to ask here is whether the demands of justice must be only about getting the institutions and rules right. Proceeding beyond them, should we not also have to examine what does emerge in the society, including the kind of lives that people can actually lead, given the institutions and rules and also other influences? The basic argument for a realization-focused understanding, for which I would argue, is that justice cannot be divorced from the actual world that emerges. Of course, institutions and rules are very important in influencing what happens, and also they are part and parcel of the actual world as well, but the realized actuality goes well beyond the organizational picture.

This is a critically important distinction in the history of theories of justice, including those in Europe and the West. But I begin with a demarcation that has a clear role in Indian intellectual debates, going back to the Sanskrit literature on the subject. Two distinct words—*niti* and *nyaya*—both of which stand for justice in classical Sanskrit, actually help us to dif-ferentiate between these two separate concentrations. It is true, of course, that words such as *niti* and *nyaya* have been used in many different senses in different philosophical and legal dis-cussions in ancient India, but there is still a basic distinction between the respective concentrations of *niti* and *nyaya*.

Among the principal uses of the term *niti* are organizational propriety and behavioural correctness. In contrast with *niti*, the term *nyaya* stand for a more comprehensive concept of realized justice. In that line of vision, the roles of institutions, rules, and organization, important as they are, have to be assessed in the broader and more inclusive perspective of *nyaya*, which is inescapably linked with the world that actually emerges, not just the institutions or rules we happen to have.

To consider an example, early Indian legal theorists talked disparagingly of what they called *matsyanyaya*, 'justice in the world of fish', where a big fish can freely devour a small fish. We are warned that avoiding *matsyanyaya* must be an overwhelming priority, and it is crucial to make sure that the 'justice of fish' is not allowed to invade the world of human beings. The central recognition here is that the realization of justice in the sense of *nyaya* is not just a matter of judging institutions and rules, but of judging societies themselves. Whatever the propriety of established organizations, if a big fish can devour a small fish at will, then that is a patent violation of human justice.

Let me consider a very simple example to make the distinction between *niti* and *nyaya* clearer. Ferdinand I, the Holy Roman emperor, famously claimed in the sixteenth century: "*Fiat justitia et pereat mundus*", which can be translated as 'Let justice be done, though the world perishes'. This severe maxim could figure as a *niti*—a very austere *niti*—that is advocated by some (indeed Emperor Ferdinand did just that), but it would be hard to accommodate a total catastrophe as an example of a just world, when we understand justice in the broader form of *nyaya*. If indeed the world does perish, there would be nothing much to admire in that accomplishment, even though the stern and severe *niti* leading to this extreme result could conceivably be defended with very sophisticated arguments of different kinds.

This distinction is also closely linked with the debate between Arjuna and Krishna in the Mahabharata. It is on the grounds of the *nyaya* of the world that would emerge from the epic battle that Arjuna voiced his profound doubts about fighting in Kurukshetra. Arjuna does not doubt that theirs is the right cause, and that this is a just war, and also that his side will definitely win the battle given its strength—not least because of Arjuna's own remarkable skills as a warrior and as an extraordinary general. But so many people, Arjuna observes, will die in this battle. Arjuna also recognizes that he himself will have to kill a great many people, and further, many of the people who will be killed, on both sides, are persons for whom he has affection.

As the account goes, Krishna argues against Arjuna and convinces him that he must do his duty, no matter what the consequence might be. When that specific section of the Mahabharata is separated out as a religious document, as it has increasingly been, in the form of the *Bhagavadgita*, or *Gita* for short, Krishna's teachings are seen as the end of the argument (Arjuna, in this understanding, had doubts, but Krishna dispelled them). But as I have discussed elsewhere, in my book *The Argumentative Indian*, looking only at the end point of a debate is not an ideal way of understanding discussions in general, and it is particularly misleading in appreciating the rich Indian argumentative tradition.

I have pursued this interpretational issue further in my foreword to the new seven-volume translation of Valmiki's Ramayana, in the Clay Sanskrit Library, which will be published shortly. I have discussed there why the social and moral contents of the epics cannot be understood adequately merely by noting who is supposed to have ended up prevailing in a particular argument—the intellectual content of the epics is much richer than that. The Mahabharata gives both Krishna and Arjuna room to develop their respective arguments. Indeed, the tragic desolation, described towards the end of the Mahabharata, that the post-combat and post-carnage land faces following the epic battle (with funeral pyres burning in massive unison and women weeping about the death of their loved ones), can even be seen as something of a vindication of Arjuna's profound doubts.

The point here is not so much to argue that Arjuna would have been definitely right to refuse to fight (there were many arguments against Arjuna's withdrawal from battle even other than the ones on which Krishna concentrated), but that there is much to weigh and balance here and that Arjuna's human-life-centred perspective is not dismissible by the mere invoking of some apparent duty to fight, irrespective of consequences. Indeed, this is a dichotomy with two substantial positions, each of which can be defended in different ways. If my own understanding of the decisional problem is strongly influenced by the *nyaya* of the realized world and the importance of human lives (and in that, I am sympathetic to Arjuna's focus on what actually happens to the people and the world), this does not indicate that I do not see the argument on the other side.

Let me now come back to the formulation of theories of justice. The subject of social justice has been discussed over the ages across the world, but the discipline received a powerful boost during the European Enlightenment, in the eighteenth and nineteenth centuries, particularly in the rebellious thoughts closely aligned in many ways to the intellectual background of the French Revolution as well as the American Revolution.

There is, however, a substantial dichotomy between the different lines of reasoning about justice among these leaders of thought. One approach concentrated on identifying perfectly just social arrangements, and took the characterization of the just institutions to be the principal—and often the only identified—task of the theory of justice. This approach, which can be called 'transcendental institutionalism' (since it looks for an ideal blueprint of social arrangements that cannot be transcended), goes back in fact to the early invocation of an idealized social contract by Thomas Hobbes in the seventeenth century, and that general approach to justice was fairly thoroughly pursued by a number of Enlightenment authors, perhaps most powerfully by Jean Jacques Rousseau and Immanuel Kant.

In contrast with that transcendental concentration, a number of other Enlightenment philosophers took a variety of approaches that shared a common interest in making comparisons between different social arrangements and realizations, and many of their arguments were particularly focused on removing cases of manifest injustice, without focusing on the nature of the perfectly just social arrangements. Different versions of such comparative thinking can be found in the works of the Marquis de Condorcet, Adam Smith, Jeremy Bentham, Mary Wollstonecraft, John Stuart Mill, Karl Marx, among a number of other leaders of new thought in the eighteenth and nineteenth centuries. Even though they proposed very different ways of making comparisons, they were all involved, in one way or another, in making social comparisons that could identify how a society could be improved and terrible injustices removed. It is possible to argue that the focus of the second group of thinkers was on the comparative assessment of the world in terms of the *nyaya* of realizations, whereas the focus of the first group was on the transcendental assessment of just arrangements, in the sense of identifying some ideal *niti* of institutions and organizations.

The distance between the two approaches—transcendental institutionalism on the one hand and realization-focused comparisons on the other—is quite momentous and large. As it happens, it is the tradition of transcendental institutionalism on which today's mainstream political philosophy largely draws in its exploration of the theory of justice. The most powerful and momentous exposition of transcendental institutionalism can be found in the works of the leading political philosopher of the twentieth century, John Rawls, but a number of other preeminent contemporary theorists of justice have also tended to take the transcendental institutional route. Indeed, the characterization of just institutions has become the central exercise in most of the modern theories of justice (Rawls's 'principles of justice' are defined entirely in institutional terms). I would argue for the need for a radical change here, since the perspective of realizations cannot but be quite central to the very idea of justice. I should not go further into those philosophical arguments here, but they are presented fairly extensively in my forthcoming book, *The Idea of Justice*, to be published in July 2009.[1]

A realization-focused perspective makes it easy to see the importance of the prevention of manifest injustice in the world, rather than focusing on the search for perfection. As the example of *matsyanyaya* makes clear, the subject of justice is not merely about trying to achieve—or dreaming about achieving—some perfectly just society or social arrangements, but about preventing manifestly severe injustice (like avoiding the dreadful state of *matsyanyaya*).

For example, when people agitated for the abolition of slavery in the eighteenth and nineteenth centuries, they were not labouring under the illusion that the abolition of slavery would make the world perfectly just. It was their claim, rather, that a society with slavery was totally unjust. That much, they argued, was absolutely clear, even if it might be very hard to identify (not to mention, achieve) a perfectly just society. Abolition of slavery was a matter of prevention of severe injustice and a significant advancement of justice; it was not meant to be an answer to the transcendental question of identifying a perfectly just society, or ideal social institutions. It was on that basis that the anti-slavery agitation, with its diagnosis of intolerable injustice, saw the pursuit of that cause to be an overwhelming priority.

That historical case can also serve as something of an analogy that is very relevant to us today in India. There are, I would argue, similarly momentous manifestations of severe injustice in our own world today in India, such as appalling levels of continued child undernourishment (almost unparalleled in the rest of the world), continuing lack of entitlement to basic medical attention of the poorer members of society, and the comprehensive absence of opportunities for basic schooling for a significant proportion of the population. Whatever else *nyaya* must demand (and we can have all sorts of different views of what a perfectly just India would look like), the reasoned humanity of the justice of *nyaya* can hardly fail to demand the urgent removal of these terrible deprivations in the world in which we actually live.

This is not only a matter for political philosophy, but also a central issue in political practice. It is easy enough to agitate about new problems that arise and generate immediate discontent, whether it is rising petrol prices or the fear of losing national sovereignty in signing a deal with another country. These too are, of course, issues of importance, but what is to me amazing is the quiet acceptance, with relatively little political murmur, of the continuation of the astounding misery of the least advantaged people of our country. The crowding out of political interest in the colossal and persistent deprivation of the underdogs of the Indian society through the dominance of more easily vocalizable current affairs (important as they may be) has a profound effect in weakening the pressure on the government to eradicate with the greatest of urgency the most gross and lasting injustice in India. There is something peculiarly puzzling about the priorities that are reflected in what seems to keep us awake at night.

Would it make a real difference whether we pay more attention to actual realizations of societies, rather than sticking to our favourite recipes about rules and institutions, be it free market, state enterprise, or support for or opposition to globalized economic relations? Is there a case for judging our favourite recipes through examining how they would influence the lives of people? And can we make the working of institutions and rules better in terms of their impact on social realizations? Let me examine just those questions, in the context of two specific institutions of rather different types: one, the social role of the trade unions in the enhancement of justice (especially for the very deprived), and two, the nature of democracy and its contribution to social justice in the actual world.

Consider the place of unions of organized workers in the social fabric of the country. It is often pointed out that only a very small proportion of the working population of India belongs to any union, and it could be asked whether it is an important enough example for me to consider as my first illustration in dealing with the distinction I am trying to discuss. The fact is, however, the life of nearly everyone in the country is affected in one way or another by the activities of unionized workers, especially in the public services, from school education and primary health care to railways and postal services.

What their rightful role should be in generating social realization is, thus, a momentous issue.

However, one difficulty in getting to the right question arises from the fact that trade unions tend to excite two quite divergent reactions, neither of which is, I would submit, very helpful. Fierce critics of unionism very often have an unconcealed disdain for the unions as just a nuisance (the less of them, the better), while others less hostile to the unions tend to treat them as being just fine—in no need of alteration—no matter how broad or narrow the goals that they pursue are. What is needed instead, it is my claim, is a kind of constructive partnership that gives the unions an integrated role as important partners in social and economic progress for people as a whole, not just to serve as watchdogs of sectional interest represented by the respective unions. At the centre of the question is the subject of the public responsibility of unionized labour linked with rightful recognition of its constructive capacity.

One of the areas that call for urgent attention in India is the efficiency of delivery of public services. That there is a large lacuna here has been brought out recently by a number of empirical studies from different parts of India, including some that we have done ourselves for the Pratichi Trust—a charitable trust I had the opportunity to set up about a decade ago with the help of my Nobel money. While our studies indicate some reason for celebration, particularly in the expansion of registration for primary schools and in the coverage of public health services, we also found a remarkably high frequency of neglect and lack of accountability in the primary schools and health services.

Consider the working of State-run elementary schools. Even though a great many primary school teachers are extremely devoted to their work and to their students, we observed a shocking incidence of absenteeism and delayed arrival on the part of many teachers in other schools. The reliance on private tuition, which should be entirely unnecessary in primary schooling, has been quite widespread among those who can afford it. The neglect of teaching responsibilities is particularly strong, we were distressed to find in our studies, when the students come mostly from underprivileged classes, for example, from families of landless labourers and very low earning workers. And this has a profound effect on the schooling of poor and underprivileged children—sometimes first-generation school-goers unsure of their rights and unable to raise their voice.

The fact that the inspection system of schools has broken down fairly comprehensively in many parts of India makes the problem harder to tackle, and there are administrative reforms that are urgently needed. However, the problem cannot be tackled by administrative changes alone.

There is a similar picture of uncertain and disparate functioning in the delivery of primary health care. The reliance of even very poor people in India on private health care providers—sometimes even medical pretenders who combine quackery with crookery—is caused not only by the lack of enough public health institutions (and that is a problem enough in itself, needing urgent expansion of facilities especially in the rural areas), but also by the poor functioning of existing public institutions for which government financing is actually available. In reforming the culture of work and in cultivating responsibility and accountability, the unions can have a hugely positive and constructive role.

I recognize that bringing about the necessary changes across the board in public sector performance through active cooperation of the unions is not an easy task. But the need for such a reorientation and change is urgent and extremely important, and it calls both for greater recognition and respect of the place of unionized labour in society, and for more deliberated determination of the unions to play their part in the progress of the country. While it is often assumed that the only responsibility of the unions is to enhance the well-being of its members, and to look after their sectional interest, the union movement across the world has, in fact, been inspired time and again by broader objectives and commitments. I believe such a change is both necessary and entirely feasible in India if we decide to pursue that line in earnest. Indeed, our limited experience in joint action with the unions entirely confirm our high expectations.

Perhaps there is too much pessimism—indeed fatalism—in India about the alleged unalterability of the working of established institutions and of behaviour patterns. Despite our lapses, which are large, our ability to respond positively to reasoned appeal and arguments remains strong enough.

I turn, finally, to democracy. We have reason to be proud of our determination to choose democracy before any other poor country in the world, and to guard jealously its survival and continued success over difficult times as well as easy ones. But democracy itself can be seen either just as an institution, with regular ballots and elections and other such organizational requirements, or it can be seen as the way things really happen in the actual world on the basis of public deliberation. I have argued in my book *The Argumentative Indian* that democracy can be plausibly seen as a system in which public decisions are taken through open public reasoning for influencing actual social states (I go more extensively into this question in the forthcoming book, *The Idea of Justice*). Something of the focus of *nyaya* on the lives that people can actually lead has to rub on to the demands on democracy itself, not leaving it all only to the *niti* of having right institutional arrangements.

Indeed, the successes and failures of democratic institutions in India can be easily linked to the way these institutions have—or have not—functioned. Take the simplest case of success (by now much discussed), namely, the elimination of the large-scale famines that India used to have right up to its independence from British rule. The fact that famines do not tend to occur in functioning democracies has been widely observed also across the world.

How does democracy bring about this result? In terms of votes and elections there may be an apparent puzzle here, since the proportion of the population affected, or even threatened, by any famine tends to be very small—typically less than 10 per cent (often far less than that). So if it were true that only disaffected famine victims vote against a ruling government when a famine rages or threatens, then the government could still be quite secure and rather unthreatened. What makes a famine such a political disaster for a ruling government is the reach of public reasoning and the role of the media, which move and energize a very large proportion of the general public to protest and shout about the 'uncaring' government when famines actually happen—or come close to happening. The achievement in preventing famines is a tribute not just to the institution of democracy, but also to the way this institution is used and made to function.

Now take some cases of lesser success—and even failure. In general, Indian democracy has been far less effective in dealing with problems of chronic deprivation and continuing inequity with adequate urgency, compared with the extreme threats of famines and other emergencies. Democratic institutions can help to create opportunities for the opposition to demand—and press for—sufficiently strong policy response even when the problem is chronic and has had a long history, rather than being acute and sudden (as in the case of famines). The weakness of Indian social policies on school education, basic health care, elementary nutrition, essential land reform, and equal treatment of women reflects, at least partly, the deficiencies of politically engaged public reasoning and the reach of political pressure.

Only in a few parts of India has the social urgency of dealing with chronic problems of deprivation been adequately politicized. It is hard to escape the general conclusion that economic performance, social opportunity, political voice, and public reasoning are deeply interrelated. In those fields in which there has recently been a more determined use of political and social voice, there are considerable signs of change. For example, the issue of gender inequality has produced much more political engagement in recent years (often led by women's movements in different fields), and while there is still a long way to go, this development has added to a determined political effort at reducing the asymmetry between women and men in terms of social and economic opportunities.

There has been more action recently in organized social movements based broadly on demands for human rights, such as the right to respect and fair treatment for members of low castes and the casteless, the right to school education for all, the right to food, the entitlement to basic health care, the right to information, the right of employment guarantee, and greater attention on environmental preservation. There is room for argument in each case about how best to proceed, and that is indeed an important role of democratic public reasoning, but we can also see clearly that social activities are an integral part of the working of democracy, which is not just about institutions such as elections and votes.

A government in a democratic country has to respond to ongoing priorities in public criticism and political reproach, and to the threats to survival it has to face. The removal of long-standing deprivations of the disadvantaged people of our country may, in effect, be hampered by the biases in political pressure, in particular when the bulk of the social agitation is dominated by new problems that generate immediate and noisy discontent among the middle class Indians with a voice. If the politically active threats are concentrated only on some specific new issues, no matter how important (such as high prices of consumer goods for the relatively rich, or the fear that India's political sovereignty might be compromised by its nuclear deal with the US), rather than on the terrible general inheritance of India of acute deprivation, deficient schooling, lack of medical attention for the poor, and extraordinary undernourishment (especially of children and also of young women), then the pressure on democratic governance acts relentlessly towards giving priority to only those particular new issues, rather than to the gigantic persistent deprivations that are at the root of so much inequity and injustice in India. The perspective of realization of justice and that of an adequately broad *nyaya* are central not only to the theory of justice, but also to the practice of democracy.

To conclude, the idea of justice links closely with the enhancement of human lives and improving the actual world in which we live, rather than taking the form, as in most mainstream theories of justice today, of some transcendental search for ideal institutions. We will not get perfect institutions, though we can certainly improve them, but no less importantly, we also have to make sure, with cooperation from all sections of the society, that these institutions work vigorously and well. Engagement with reasons of justice is particularly critical in identifying the overwhelming priorities that we have to acknowledge and overcome with total urgency. A good first step is to think more clearly—and far more often—about what should really keep us awake at night.

Reference

1. Amartya Sen, *The Idea of Justice* (London: Allen Lane, 2009).

WHAT DIFFERENCE CAN
TAGORE MAKE?

In his book *Raga Mala*, Ravi Shankar, the great musician, argues that had Rabindranath Tagore "been born in the West he would now be [as] revered as Shakespeare and Goethe." This is, of course, a strong claim, and it draws attention to some greatness in this quintessentially Bengali writer that is identified by a fellow Bengali, Ravi Shankar, which might not be readily echoed in the wider world today, especially in the West. For the Bengali public, Tagore has been, and remains, an altogether exceptional literary figure, towering over all others. His poems, songs, novels, short stories, critical essays, and other writings have vastly enriched the cultural environment in which hundreds of millions of people live in the Bengali-speaking world, whether in Bangladesh or in India. Something of that glory is acknowledged in India outside Bengal as well, and even in some other parts of Asia (including China and Japan), but in the rest of the world, especially in Europe and America, Tagore clearly is not a big name.

And yet the enthusiasm and excitement that Tagore's writings created in the early years of the twentieth century in Europe and America were quite remarkable. *Gitanjali*, a selection of his poems for which Rabindranath was awarded the Nobel Prize in literature in 1913, was published in English translation in London in March 1913 and had been reprinted 10 times by November when the award was announced. For many years Tagore was something of a rage in many European countries, and his meetings were always overpacked with people wanting to hear him. But then, what can be called the Tagore tide ebbed, and by the 1930s the huge excitement was all over. Indeed, by 1937, Graham Greene was able to remark, "As for Rabindranath Tagore, I cannot believe that anyone but Mr Yeats can still take his poems very seriously."

The 150th anniversary of Rabindranath's birth is a good occasion to ask what happened. Given the fairly comprehensive neglect of this author in contemporary English literature, it could well be asked why a writer who evokes comparison, in a seasoned assessment, with Shakespeare and Goethe tends to generate so little enthusiasm in Western countries today. There is surely some mystery there.

At one level it is not particularly hard to see that his native readers can get something from Tagore's writings, especially poems and songs, that would be missed by those who do not read Bengali. Even his biggest promoter in the English-speaking world, W.B. Yeats, did not like Tagore's own English translations. "Tagore does not know English," Yeats declared, adding a little theory to that diagnosis (as he often did), "no Indian knows English." And Yeats was very willing to work with Tagore to overcome that perceived handicap in the production of the English version of *Gitanjali*.

There are, in fact, some serious problems with Yeats-assisted translations as well (on which more later), but the more general obstacle surely comes from the fact that poetry is notoriously difficult to translate. Even with the best of effort and talent, it can be very hard—if not impossible—to preserve the magic of poetry as it is transplanted from one language to another. Anyone who knows Tagore's poems in original Bengali would typically find it hard to be really satisfied with any translation, no matter how good. To that has to be added the fact that many of Tagore's poems, which take the form of songs in an innovative style of lyrical singing—what is called 'Rabindrasangeet'—has transformed popular Bengali music with its particular combination of reflective language and compatible tunes.

There is, in addition, the problem that Tagore's influence on Bengali writing was so gigantic and epoch-making that his innovative language itself has profound importance to the Bengali reading public. Kazi Nazrul Islam, almost certainly the most successful Bengali poet with the exception of Tagore, was constantly expressing his admiration of the person he called, uniquely, 'the world poet'. Nazrul also argued that Tagore had altogether transformed the Bengali language. Indeed, in many different ways, Tagore has, through his writings, been able to reshape and reconstruct modern Bengali, in a way that only a handful of innovative Bengali writers had done before him, going back all the way, a thousand years before Rabindranath, to the authors of *Charyapada*, the Buddhist literary classics that first established the distinctive features of early modern Bengali. Tagore's impact on Bengali prose, though perhaps a little less than on Bengali poetry, was immensely strong as well.

Not only is language a part of the story in the contrast between Tagore's appreciation at home and indifference abroad, but a related component of the story lies in the extraordinary importance and unusual place of language in

Bengali culture in general. It is worth noting here that the Bengali language has had an amazingly powerful influence on the identity of Bengalis as a group, on both sides of the political boundary between Bangladesh and India. In fact, the politically separatist campaign in what was East Pakistan that led to the war for independence and eventually the formation of the new secular state of Bangladesh, was pioneered by the '*bhasha andolan*'—the 'language movement'—in defence of the Bengali language.

The movement started in the early 1950s, only a few years after the Partition of the subcontinent, with a major demonstration on 21 February 1952, which turned out to be a decisive moment in the history of what would later become Bangladesh. 21 February is celebrated every year in Bangladesh as the Language Movement Day, and has been declared by the UNESCO as the International Mother Language Day for the whole world. Language has served as a very powerful uniting identity of Muslims and Hindus in Bengal, and that sense of shared belonging has had a profound impact on the politics of Bengal, including its commitment to secularism on both sides of the border in the post-Partition world.

The extraordinary combination of Rabindranath's language and themes has had a captivating influence on his Bengali readers. Many Bengalis express their astonishment at the fact that people outside Bengal could fail to appreciate and enjoy Tagore's writings (there are also some fine conspiracy theories that flourish—some more hair-raising than others), and that incomprehension is at least partly due to underestimating the big difference that language can make. E.M. Forster noted the barrier of language, as early as 1919, when Tagore was still a rage, in reviewing the translation of one of Tagore's great Bengali novels, *Ghare Baire*, translated into English as *The Home and the World* (later it would be made into an outstanding film by Satyajit Ray). Forster confessed that he could not make himself like the English version of the novel he read. "The theme is so beautiful," he remarked, but the charms have "vanished in translation."

The importance of language provides undoubtedly one clue to the eclipse of Tagore in the West. But that cannot be the whole story. For one thing, Tagore's non-fictional prose writings also have a gripping hold on the attention of the Bengalis and also of other Indians, but they are not seen abroad in a similarly admiring way at all. This is so, despite the fact that these writings are much easier to translate than either poetry or fiction is (indeed Tagore himself often presented these essays in English, in fact in very effective English about which it would be hard to grumble). Tagore presented his general ideas on a remarkably wide variety of subjects—on politics, on culture, on science, on society, on education—and while these essays and lectures are regularly quoted in his homeland, they are very rarely invoked now outside Bangladesh and India. There has to be something other than the barrier of language in the lack of attention to Tagore outside Bangladesh and India.

This raises the general question: how relevant, how important are Tagore's general ideas? And that is a really engaging issue to face in celebrating Tagore's birth anniversary. I shall concentrate on that question for its own importance, rather than for what it tells us about possible reasons for the difference in the assessment of Tagore at home and abroad.

However, I shall briefly return to the 'whodunit' towards the end of this essay.

Perhaps the central issues that moved Tagore most are the importance of open-minded reasoning and the celebration of human freedom. This placed Rabindranath Tagore in a somewhat distinct category from some of his great compatriots. For example, Tagore admired Mahatma Gandhi immensely, expressed his admiration of his leadership time and again, and did more than perhaps anyone else in insisting that he be described as 'Mahatma'—the great soul. And yet Tagore frequently disagreed with Gandhi, whenever he thought Gandhiji was departing from adequate reasoning, and the two would often argue with each other quite emphatically. When, for example, Gandhiji used the catastrophic Bihar earthquake of 1934 that killed a huge number of people as a further ammunition in his fight against untouchability (Gandhi identified the earthquake as "a divine chastisement sent by God for our sins"—in particular the sin of untouchability), Tagore protested vehemently, adding, "It is all the more unfortunate because this kind of unscientific view of phenomena is too readily accepted by a large section of our countrymen."

To give another example, when Gandhiji advocated that everyone should use the *charkha*—the primitive spinning wheel—30 minutes a day (he saw the *charkha*, which became very closely associated with Gandhiji, both as the basis of his alternative economics as well as a great way of personal upliftment),

Tagore expressed his disagreement sharply. Rabindranath thought little of Gandhiji's version of alternative economics, finding reason to celebrate, with a few qualifications, the liberating role of modern technology in reducing human drudgery as well as poverty. And he also was deeply sceptical of the upliftment argument: "The *charkha* does not require anyone to think; one simply turns the wheel of the antiquated invention endlessly, using the minimum of judgment and stamina." Similarly, in contrast with Gandhiji's advocacy of abstinence as the right method of birth control, Tagore championed family planning through preventive methods. Tagore was also concerned that Gandhiji had "a horror of sex as great as that of the author of *The Kreutzer Sonata*", and further, the two differed sharply on the role of modern medicine, to which Gandhi was not friendly at all.

Many of these issues remain deeply relevant even today. But what is important to note here is not the particular views that Tagore advanced in these and other such areas, but the organizing principles that moved him, which were guided by the necessity of critical reasoning and the importance of human freedom. These priorities influenced Tagore's ideas on education, including his insistence that education is the most important element in the development of a country. In his assessment of Japan's economic development, Tagore separated out the role that the advancement of school education had played in Japan's remarkable development—an analysis that would be echoed much later in the standard literature on economic development. Tagore may have been exaggerating the role of education somewhat when he remarked, "The imposing tower of misery which today rests on the heart of India has its sole foundation in the absence of education," but it is not hard to see why he saw the transformative role of education as the central story in the development process.

Rabindranath devoted much of his life to advancing education in India and advocating it everywhere. Nothing absorbed as much of his time as the school he had established in Santiniketan. He was constantly raising money for this unusually progressive co-educational school. I have to declare a bias here, since I was educated there (my mother too had been schooled there, decades earlier, in what was one of the early co-educational institutions in India). Immediately after learning in November 1913 that he had been chosen for the award of the Nobel Prize in literature, Tagore told others about it, the story goes, in a meeting of a school committee discussing how to fund a new set of drains that the school needed. His announcement of the news of the Nobel Prize apparently took the eccentric form of saying, "Money for the drains has probably been found."

In his distinctive view of education, Tagore particularly emphasized the need for gathering knowledge from everywhere in the world, assessed only by reasoned scrutiny. As a student at the Santiniketan school, I felt very privileged that the geographic boundaries of our education were not confined only to India and imperial Britain, but we learned a great deal about Europe and Africa and Latin America, and even more extensively about other countries in Asia. Santiniketan had the first institute of Chinese studies in India; my mother had learned Judo in the school nearly a century ago; and there were excellent training facilities in arts, crafts, and music from other countries, like batik and shadow theatre from Indonesia.

Rabindranath also worked hard to break out of religious and communal thinking that was beginning to get some championing in India during his lifetime—it would peak in the years following his death in 1941 when the Hindu–Muslim riots suddenly erupted in the subcontinent, making the partitioning of the country hard to avoid. Tagore was extremely shocked by the violence that drew on the singular identity of people as members of one religion or another, and he felt convinced that the cultivated disaffection was being fostered on a normally tolerant people by political instigators: "interested groups led by ambition and outside instigation, are today using the communal motive for destructive political ends."

Tagore became more and more anxious and disappointed about India and about the world shortly preceding his death, and he did not live to see the emergence of either an independent, secular India or a secular Bangladesh. Drawing inspiration from Tagore's firm rejection of communal separatism, Bangladesh chose one of Tagore's songs (*Amar sonar Bangla*) as its national anthem, making Tagore possibly the only person in human history who had authored the national anthems of two independent countries, since India had already adopted another song of Tagore (*Jana gana mana adhinayaka*) as its national anthem.

All this must be very confusing to those who see the contemporary world as a 'clash of civilizations'—with 'the Muslim civilization', 'the Hindu civilization', and 'the Western civilization', defined largely on religious grounds, vehemently confronting each other. They would also be confused by Rabindranath Tagore's description of his own cultural background: "a confluence of three cultures, Hindu, Mohammedan and British". Rabindranath's grandfather, Dwarkanath, was well-known for his command over Arabic and Persian, and Rabindranath grew up in a family atmosphere in which a deep knowledge of Sanskrit and ancient texts—religious and literary—was combined with the learning of Islamic traditions as well as Persian literature. It is not so much that Rabindranath tried to produce—or had an interest in producing—a 'synthesis' of the different religions (as the great Mughal emperor Akbar had tried hard to achieve), but his reliance on reasoning and his emphasis on human freedom militated against a separatist and parochial understanding of social divisions.

If Tagore's voice was strong against communalism and religious sectarianism, he was no less outspoken in his rejection of nationalism. He was critical of the display of excessive nationalism in India, despite his persistent criticism of British imperialism. And despite his great admiration for Japanese culture and history, he would chastise Japan late in his life for its extreme nationalism and its mistreatment of China and of people in East and Southeast Asia.

Tagore also went out of his way to dissociate the criticism of the Raj from any denunciation of British people and culture. Consider Mahatma Gandhi's famous witticism in reply to the question, asked in England, about what he thought of British civilization: Gandhi had said, "It would be a good idea." There are some doubts about the authenticity of the story, but whether or not exactly accurate, the remark did fit with Gandhiji's amused scepticism of British greatness; but those words could not have come from Rabindranath's lips, even in jest. While he denied altogether the legitimacy of the Raj, Rabindranath was vocal in pointing out what India had gained from "discussions centred upon Shakespeare's drama and Byron's poetry and above all ... the large-hearted liberalism of nineteenth-century English politics." The tragedy, as Tagore saw it, came from the fact that what "was truly best in their own civilization, the upholding of the dignity of human relationships, has no place in the British administration of this country."

Tagore saw the world in terms of a huge give and take of ideas and innovations. He insisted that "whatever we understand and enjoy in human products instantly becomes ours, wherever they might have their origin." He went on to proclaim, "I am proud of my humanity when I can acknowledge the poets and artists of other countries as my own. Let me feel with unalloyed gladness that all the great glories of man are mine."

The importance of these ideas has not diminished in the divisive world in which we live. If that at least partly answers the question 'What difference can Tagore make?' it also puts into sharper focus the strangeness of the eclipse of Tagore in the West after an initial outburst of enthusiasm. I end with a few remarks on that.

In explaining what happened to Tagore in the West, it is important to see the one-sided way in which Rabindranath's

Western admirers had presented him. This was partly related to the priorities of Tagore's principal sponsors in Europe, such as W.B. Yeats and Ezra Pound. As I have discussed in my essay 'Tagore and His India' published in *The New York Review of Books* in 1997, both were dedicated to placing Tagore in the light of a mystical religiosity that went sharply against the overall balance of Tagore's works. In Yeats's case, his presentational priority included his adding explanatory remarks to the translation of Tagore's poems to make sure that the reader got the 'main' religious point, eliminating altogether the rich ambiguity of meaning in Tagore's language between love of human beings and love of God.

However, a part of the answer of the puzzle can, I would argue, be found in the peculiar position in which Europe was placed when Tagore's poems became such a rage in the West. Tagore received his Nobel Prize in December 1913, very shortly before the start of the First World War (1914–18), which was fought in Europe with unbelievable brutality. The barbarity and killings in the First World War had made many intellectuals and literary figures in Europe turn to insights coming from elsewhere, and Tagore's voice seemed to many, at that time, to fit the need splendidly. When, for example, the pocket book of Wilfred Owen, the great anti-war poet, was recovered from the battlefield in which he had died, his mother, Susan Owen, found in it a prominent display of Tagore's poetry. The poem of Tagore with which Wilfred had said good-bye before leaving for the battlefield (it began, 'When I go from hence, let this be my parting word') was very much there, as Susan wrote to Rabindranath, with those words "written in his dear writing—with your name beneath."

Tagore soon became identified in Europe as something of a sage with a message—a message that could, quite possibly, save Europe from the dire predicament of war and disaffection in which it recurrently found itself in the early twentieth century. This was a far cry from the many-sided creative artist and reasoned thinker that people at home found in Tagore. Even as Tagore urged his countrymen to reject blind belief and to rely instead on critical and diligent use of reasoning, Yeats was describing Tagore's voice in thoroughly mystical terms: "we have met our own image ... or heard, perhaps for the first time in literature, our voice as in a dream." There is a huge gulf there, with major consequences on the Western reading of Rabindranath.

Tagore argued for the courage to depart from traditional beliefs whenever reasoning demanded that. There is a nice little short story of Tagore, called '*Kartar bhoot*' ('The Ghost of the Leader'), illustrating this point. A wise and highly respected leader who received unquestioned admiration from a community had become, in effect, a tyrant while he lived, and enormously more so after his death. The story describes how ridiculously restrained people's lives became when the dead leader's past recommendations got frozen into inflexible commands, without his being able to offer any exceptions. Traumatized by their impossibly difficult lives, the members of the group pray to the dead leader to liberate them from their bondage. In reply, the leader reminds them that he exists only in their minds and they are free to liberate themselves whenever they wished. Tagore had a real horror of being bound by the past, beyond the reach of present reasoning.

However, Tagore himself did not do much to resist the wrongly conceived greatness as a mystical sage that was being thrust upon him. Even though he wrote to his friend C.F. Andrews in 1920 at the height of his adulation as an Eastern messiah, "These people ... are like drunkards who are afraid of their lucid intervals," he seemed to play along without much public protest. There was perhaps some tension within Tagore's self-perception which had allowed him to entertain the belief that the East had a real message to give to the West, and this conviction fitted rather badly with the rest of Tagore's reasoned commitments and convictions. There was also a serious mismatch between the kind of religiosity that the Western intellectuals, led by Tagore's sponsors like Yeats and Pound, came to attribute to Tagore (Graham Greene thought that he had seen in Tagore 'the bright pebbly eyes' of the Theosophists), and the open-minded, liberal form that Tagore's beliefs—religious and others—actually had.

Tagore's religious inclinations are perhaps best represented by one of his poems (I am taking the liberty of translating the lines into simple English, away from the Biblical English that Tagore had been persuaded to use):

> Leave this chanting and singing and telling of beads!
> Whom do you worship in this lonely dark corner of a temple
> with doors all shut?
> Open your eyes and see your God is not before you!
> He is there where the tiller is tilling the hard ground
> and where the path-maker is breaking stones.
> He is with them in sun and in shower,
> and his garment is covered with dust.

Even though an unalienated God, who is not a source of fear but of love, has a big role in Tagore's thinking, he is guided on all worldly questions not by any kind of mysticism but by explicit and discernible reasoning. That real Tagore got very little attention from his Western audience—neither from his sponsors (who championed Tagore's alleged mysticism), nor from his detractors (who shunned Tagore). Bertrand Russell wrote (these were letters to Nimai Chatterjee in the 1960s) that he did not like Tagore's "mystic air", with an inclination to air "vague nonsense" (adding that the "sort of language that is admired by many Indians unfortunately does not mean anything at all"). When an otherwise sympathetic writer like Bernard Shaw transformed Rabindranath Tagore into a fictional character of extreme oddity called Stupendranath Begorr, there was not much hope that Tagore's reasoned ideas would receive the attention they deserved.

In contrast, Tagore's vision of the future of his country and, in fact, of the world, there was much emphasis on reasoning and much celebration of freedom, precisely the subjects on which more discussion can have an enormously constructive role today. In a moving poem, Tagore outlined his vision for his own country and the whole world:

> Where the mind is without fear and the head is held high
> Where knowledge is free
> Where the world has not been broken up into fragments
> By narrow domestic walls.

The force of Tagore's ideas, which was deeply appreciated and influential at home, failed to penetrate the barriers of preconception and prejudice that incarcerated him in an odd little box in the West.

The difficulty in Tagore's reception in the West itself can perhaps be seen as a particular illustration of a world 'broken up into fragments by narrow domestic walls'. The fragmentary distortions take distinct forms in different societies and in different contexts, and in arguing for a world in which 'the mind is without fear and the head is held high', Tagore wanted to overcome all these barriers. He did not quite succeed there. Yet engagement in open-minded and fearless reasoning, so strongly championed by Rabindranath, is no less important today than it was in his own time.

Notes and References

1. *The Essential Tagore*, Fakrul Alam and Radha Chakravarty (eds) (Harvard University Press, 2011).

2. 'The "Foreign Reincarnation" of Rabindranath Tagore', by Nabaneeta Dev Sen, *Journal of Asian Studies*, volume 25 (Cambridge University Press, 1966); reprinted, along with other relevant papers, in her *Counterpoints: Essays in Comparative Literature* (Calcutta: Prajna, 1985).

3. *Selected Letters of Rabindranath Tagore*, Krishna Dutta and Andrew Robinson (eds) (Cambridge: Cambridge University Press, 1997). See also the same editors' *Rabindranath Tagore: The Myriad-Minded Man* (New York: St. Martin's Press, 1995), and *Rabindranath Tagore: An Anthology* (Picador, 1997).

A WISH A DAY FOR A WEEK

Speech delivered at the ZEE Jaipur Literature Festival, Diggi Palace, Jaipur, on 17 January 2014.

On being invited to the Jaipur Festival, I was naturally nervous about attempting an opening address to such an elite gathering. However, about ten days ago I saw in the newspapers, indeed in all of them, that India has entered triumphantly into the 'elite club' of the world. *The Times of India*'s headline said: "GSLV-DV Launch Successful, India Joins Elite Club." As an Indian citizen, I immediately lost all fear about not being able to get into the elite club. However, I had a problem in not knowing what GSLV-DV is. Or does. On probing I found that GSLV-DV is famous because it carries a GSAT-14 communication satellite. That seemed just what I needed. And so I decided to use the GSAT-14 communication satellite to communicate well beyond my station in life.

High above the clouds I came across a figure who looked very impressive, who explained that she was the Goddess of Medium Things. "Gosh," I said. "Medium you may be, but you look very impressive." "You should see," she replied, "the Goddess of *Large* Things." "You could please introduce me to her," I said, "but are you sure that you are really a goddess?" "Yes I am," she responded firmly, "I am—as I told you—Goddess of Medium Things. But, you are right, I am very informal, and you can call me GMT—that is my pet name." "Isn't GMT some kind of time?" I asked her. "Yes," she said, "I can give you the correct time, also one of my specialties, but more importantly I can grant you a wish—in fact more than one wish—for your country." "How jolly," I said, "May I have seven wishes—a wish a day for my country for a week? Please, let us get on with it!"

"Sure," GMT said, "but why are you in such a hurry?" I explained, "I am going to the Jaipur Literature Festival. You have heard of the famous Jaipur Literature Festival, my goddess?" "Yes," GMT said, "but it is really so big now that it has been moved from my care to the care of the Goddess of *Large* Things. Still, I will try to help you. Make a medium-sized wish about literature."

So I jumped in: "Classical education in language, literature, music, and the arts are being seriously neglected in India. Very few people study Sanskrit anymore. Nor do they study ancient Persian, or Latin, or Greek, or Arabic, or Hebrew, or Old Tamil. We need serious cultivation of classical studies for a balanced education. In India's increasingly business-oriented society, there is generally far less room today for the humanities, and that is surely a problem, is it not, goddess?" "But," said the goddess, "Rabindranath Tagore in your village, Santiniketan, used to grumble that science education was being neglected. So how can you say the opposite?" "That was then, madam," I said, "and this is now. Rabindranath was right in his day, but bright students now, everywhere in India, go for science and technology, and look down on humanities."

"So," asked the goddess, "you wish to have a greater role of humanities in Indian education?" "Something like that," I said. "What a vague statement: 'something like that!'" GMT said, "you must have clearer ideas." "Clearer? Do you mean more precise, dear goddess?" I asked. "No," said GMT, "you are making the common mistake of assuming that a clear statement needs to invoke precise magnitudes. A good statement of an inherently imprecise concern—and most important concerns in the world are imprecise—must *capture* that imprecision, and not replace it by a precise statement about something else. You should learn to speak in an articulate way about ideas that are inescapably imprecise (as a man called Aristotle put it more than two millennia ago). And that is one of the reasons why the humanities are important. A novel can point to a truth without pretending to capture it exactly in some imagined numbers and formulae. Okay then, now go on to your second wish."

"Well," I said, "may I go into politics?" GMT looked unsurprised and said, "I think I can guess what you are going to ask, knowing your left-wing views—you are on the left in India, aren't you?" "Nothing escapes you, goddess," I replied, "I am. But my big political wish is to have a strong and flourishing *right-wing* party that is secular and not communal." "Why?" asked a slightly puzzled goddess. "There is an important role," I explained, "for a clear-headed pro-market, pro-business party that does not depend on religious politics, and does not prioritize one religious community over all others." GMT said, "Surely there was such a party in India, led by some very smart people, wasn't there?" I said, "Yes, madam, there was—it was called the Swatantra Party, and among its leaders was Minoo Masani, an extremely smart fellow indeed—but the party died. I wish it would be revived." "Let me recollect," GMT said, "this Minoo Masani—was he really in favour of non-communal politics and did he believe in the brotherhood of all people, what the French revolutionaries call 'fraternity'? I seem to recollect that he said some unflattering things about fraternity in one of his public speeches." "Yes, goddess," I told GMT, "he was staunchly secular and very much in favour of fraternity. But in a light-hearted remark in 1946, Masani said that he adored fraternity but given the misuses of the word after French Revolution, he did not use it. He went on to say in the Constituent Assembly of India on 17 December 1946, 'When I introduce my brother, I call him my cousin.'"

"Would that be your favourite party then?" asked the goddess. "No, absolutely not," I said. "But I would very much like such a party to be there, giving Indian voters the choice of supporting a secular, pro-business point of view—it would be very good for Indian politics. The support that a right-wing pro-business point of view receives should not have to be parasitic on making an alliance with religious politics."

"Okay," said GMT, "but can you make your explanations short—we don't have much time. Let me remind you that you are speaking to me and not lecturing at the Jaipur Festival. What's your third wish?" "I would like the parties of the left to be stronger, but also more clear-minded and much more concentrated on removing severe deprivations of the really poor and downtrodden people of India." "But what about the priority that is attached to their dedication to fighting against American imperialism?" GMT enquired—and then went on, "Now that the Soviet Union is gone, the Chinese are beating the Americans in the market economy, the Latin Americans and the Vietnamese are racing ahead with their own economic and social progress, surely the Indian Left is the only remaining political group in the world on whom the mantle of fighting American imperialism has fallen. And in giving priority to their dedicated pursuit of that philosophical priority, they have made various Parliamentary moves that have reduced the number of seats they themselves have in Parliament. It is not easy for me to make them politically stronger until they themselves think afresh."

"I hope they will," I said. "What the left really has to concentrate on is reversing the terrible state of the really poor people of India, rather than nursing an antiquated understanding of imperialism, or joining the other political parties in agitating for cheaper amenities for parts of the middle classes." "Another lecture!" said GMT, "But I am a patient goddess, and ready to listen to your grumble about your own friends; so go on—what's the fourth wish?"

"I would like the media to be more responsive to the needs of the poorest people, and less single-minded in their coverage of the world of glitzy entertainment and shining business opportunities. They are right to grumble about the way subsidies waste economic resources, but largely fail to denounce subsidies for the better off, in the way subsidies for the unemployed and the hungry are savaged in the press. Reading the papers or listening to media on fiscal irresponsibility of supporting employment schemes and food subsidies, you would scarcely guess that many times as much governmental money is spent on subsidizing electricity for those who are lucky enough to have power connection (a third of the Indian people have no connections at all), subsidizing diesel, cheapening fertilizers, offering low-cost cooking gas (most Indians have no instruments into which these inputs would go) than on supporting food and employment schemes for the poor. The latest figures are the following: subsidies on food 0.85 per cent of GDP and employment guarantee scheme (NREGA) cost 0.29 per cent of GDP. Compared with that the power subsidies, in various forms, for those who have electric connections amount altogether to more than one full percentage of the GDP, possibly closer to 2 per cent, to which should be added 0.66 per cent on fertilizer subsidy and 0.97 per cent on petroleum subsidy (diesel, cooking gas, etc.). So the much criticized food subsidy and employment guarantee for the poor and the unemployed cost about 1.14 per cent of GDP, whereas the cost of subsidizing electricity, fuel, and fertilizers for the relatively better off is minimally 2.63 per cent, and possibly closer to 3.63 per cent of GDP—more than three times what is allocated to feed the poor and provide employment to the unemployed.

"Yet," I continued, "reading the papers and hearing broadcasts you would tend to think that it is subsidy for the poor—food and employment—that strains India's public resources, even though two to three times as much governmental funds are spent in subsidizing the better off. In fact, since the government spends only a miserable 1.2 per cent of the GDP on health care (unlike in China where the percentage is nearer 3 per cent) the total government expenditure on health (in all forms), food subsidies, and employment subsidy is much less than what the government spends on subsidizing the consumption of power, diesel, cooking gas, fertilizers, etc., for the relatively rich—and much more vocal—people.

"It is sad that the most vibrant media in the world is so silent on the needs and predicaments of the poorest. A third of Indians have no electric connections. The media made such a fuss—quite rightly in its context—about 600 million people not having power on a day in July two years ago when there was a terrible administrative bungle about power supply, but neglected to report the fact that 200 million of those 600 million people never had any power at all—a perpetual blackout—because they were not even connected to electricity."

"Enough, enough," said the goddess, "go on." "My fifth wish is easy to speak about," I said, "since it concerns persistent deprivations I have been nagging about for decades: all children must have decent schools to go to; every person must have medical care beginning with preventative care; women should not have to lead more deprived lives than men; the country should not be full of undernourished children (not to mention the most undernourished in the world); every child has to be fully immunized (rather than a third of the children being left out); everyone should have a home with a toilet (rather than half the population having to defecate in the open, even as India supposedly joins the elite club of the world); and there should be generally good higher education and a sustainable environment." GMT said, "You ask for a list of different things as parts of one wish. However, I will not be small-minded, since I am medium-hearted.

"But all that you have asked for should be very easy to achieve if your countrymen start making intelligent use of the resources that economic growth generates. And this will work both ways: the advancement of human abilities resulting from these supportive changes will, in turn, help to sustain high economic growth in long run because nothing, ultimately, is more important for economic growth than having a healthy and educated labour force (ask the Chinese, Japanese, Koreans, and other Asians and they will tell you). That is the biggest lesson of East Asian development that India has missed."

"Since we agree on that, may I put in a wish, dear goddess," I said, "which concerns a peculiar judicial decision in India, which has recently recriminalized homosexual personal behaviour. The British rulers had made that a criminal offence in 1861, and made many people vulnerable to blackmail by the police and to penalization. That Article 377 of the Penal Code was overturned by the Delhi High Court as being contrary to personal rights guaranteed by the Indian constitution, but then the Indian Supreme Court—represented by exactly two judges—has reversed the reversal, and made a strictly private behaviour, once again, a social crime. Can you reverse the reversal of the reversal, dear goddess?" "Let me see," said the goddess, "How I can persuade the Indian Supreme Court to think again—maybe they will listen more to the voices of the Indian people than to the plea of a goddess above the clouds.

"Let's go on," continued GMT. "Do you really want another wish?" "May I? I wish we in India will recognize our strength because of the nature of the country as well as the opportunities given by India's democracy, which has been skilfully used recently by Aam Aadmi Party (even though they have a lot to learn about on what their programmes should really be). We have a lot of corruption, but it has become a major electoral issue, which, in a democracy, is the best way for a long-run solution, which will require many administrative reforms. But there are many achievements already, and it is not the case that nothing happens here other than what the business community does, and the state, in particular, cannot achieve anything (as many people go on repeating). India was the country of famines until the empire ended, and we haven't had a real famine since Independence; thanks to public action, India was expected a few years ago to have the largest concentration of the AIDS epidemic, but the public attention and social engagement has removed that threat. Since polio eradication became a politically sensitive issue, things have happened and India is now polio-free. We had a super-cyclone in the fall coming from the Bay of Bengal, many times the size of Katrina in the USA, but the government moved a million people off the coast in good time, and the predicted disaster did not happen. Even though India's record of social achievements is low, wherever they have tried hard to make a change—like in Kerala, Tamil Nadu, and Himachal Pradesh—education and health care have surged ahead and so have economic growth, so that these erstwhile poor states are now among India's richest. We can do things if we put our mind to it.

"Take gender inequality," I went on. "There is a lot of attention that is right now being given to the incidence of rape in India, which is an improvement. But some recognitions are missing still. The reported rate of rapes in India is low (it is 1.8 per 100,000 in India compared with 27 per 100,000 in the USA and 29 in UK). There is surely a huge underestimation here, particularly when the victims come from the poorer and less privileged classes. But even after raising the Indian number ten-fold, the rate of rape in India would still be lower than UK, USA, and most countries in the world. The main problem is not the high incidence of rape in India, but the difficulty in getting the police to cooperate and help victims, and for the society to take greater interest in sexual assaults on vulnerable women, particularly from the poorer and less-privileged classes and castes. Some steps are being taken right now to change this, including stopping sexual trafficking of girls from very poor families. But much more needs to be done, and indeed can be done if we try.

"People are very worried—and rightly—that selective abortion of female foetuses is so common and makes the female–male ratio at birth much lower in India as a whole than in the range for European countries. But nearly half the Indian states—in fact all the states in south and the east in India (from Kerala and Tamil Nadu all the way to West Bengal and Assam)—have female–male ratios at birth that are well within the European range, and it is the fact that all the states in north and west have much lower female–male ratios than in Europe that makes the Indian average come out to be so low. So there is much to learn from within India itself. Can you help in this, GMT, in making Indians less defeatist?" I asked.

"I can't do that," said the goddess, "it has to be the Indians who change their defeatist mindset." "That's a let-down," I said with frustration. "Not at all," remarked the goddess. "I am telling you that you can solve these problems yourself—you don't need anybody's help. You have to know what the problems are, and how they can be solved." "But," I complained, "even if it becomes clear what our problems are and how they can be solved, how can we share this knowledge, and make all Indians take an interest in our real problems?" "Well," said GMT, "the social media can help, and—very importantly—you must read more books.

"And," GMT added, "the time has come for you to go to the Jaipur Festival—good reading!" As the good goddess suddenly vanished beyond the clouds, I returned to my little GSAT-14, launched by the world famous GSLV-DV, to come straight to the festival. And I am grateful that you are all here. Thank You!

ON NALANDA UNIVERSITY

W hen classes began in the newly re-established ancient university of Nalanda—the oldest in the world—it was a good moment for the history of higher education. The event got attention across the world—not least in Italy, which is proud to have the oldest university in Europe, located in Bologna, established in AD 1088. By that time, however, the university in Nalanda, founded in the early fifth century, had already been functioning for more than 600 years—educating thousands of students each year. Italy's largest selling newspaper, *Corriere della Sera*, carried a glowing report on the revival of the much older Indian university in a report with the headline '*Ritorno a Nalanda*'.

If it was an occasion for academic celebration in the world, it was, for me personally, also a deeply nostalgic moment. I recalled the time—nearly 70 years ago—when, as an impressionable child, I stared with awe at the remains of the old Nalanda, and wondered whether that great university could ever come to life again. "Is it really gone forever?" I asked my grandfather, Pundit Kshiti Mohan Sen, who was also my Sanskrit teacher and my first educator in history. "Perhaps not," said the old man who always generated such cultural optimism, "it can do us a lot of good today."

Old Nalanda

When classes were held in Nalanda more than 1,500 years ago, it was the only institution of higher learning in the world offering instruction of a kind that we now expect from universities around the globe. Nalanda broke completely new ground, and established itself as a distinguished academic institution offering advanced education in a great many fields. It gradually became what we now call a university. It drew students not only from all over India, but also from China and Japan and Korea and other Asian countries with Buddhist connections, and by the seventh century it had ten thousand residential students. Nalanda offered education not only in Buddhist studies, but also in a variety of academic subjects, including languages and literatures, astronomy and observational sciences, architecture and sculpture, and medicine and public health care. The world—not just India—needed a university like that; and in a totally original way, Nalanda came into existence and grew from strength to strength. It attracted students from half the ancient world. As the excavations of the old ruins bring out—both in Nalanda and in neighbouring areas in Bihar in which educational institutions were springing up, inspired by the example of Nalanda—it was bringing in something of value to the world which did not exist earlier.

There was, of course, the justly famous Buddhist educational centre in Takshashila at the western end of ancient India (now in Pakistan), next to neighbouring Afghanistan. But the institution in Taxila, as it is often called, was really a religious school—a very distinguished one for that rather narrower engagement. There was certainly no dearth of scholarship at the eastern edge of Afghanistan and adjacent ancient India (they were culturally integrated), and even the greatest—and the earliest—Indian grammarian, the redoubtable Panini in the fourth century BC, came from the border of Afghanistan.

However, Taxila did not try to offer systematic instruction on different branches of advanced learning (particularly on secular subjects), as Nalanda and its followers in Bihar—Vikramshila, Odantapuri, and others—did, in what can be broadly described as the Nalanda-inspired world of higher education. It does not diminish the glory of Taxila, in its own context, to recognize Nalanda as the oldest university in the world.

I have to confess that despite my personal involvement with Nalanda from the age of 11, when I first visited Nalanda with wonder and admiration, it was striking for me to see the excavations going on in Telhara (near Nalanda) and the process of unearthing lecture halls and student hostels from more than a thousand years ago in a way that was completely unique to Bihar. The last thing we might, in general, expect to see as we excavate old historical ruins is a set of large halls, usable—and presumably used—for lectures and instructions, and clusters of small bedrooms, usable—and presumably used—as hostels for students. And yet, amidst a plethora of other objects—utensils, statues, lamps, ornaments, and icons—these are exactly what emerged as the diggings proceeded. Since I was born in a university campus and have spent nearly all my life in one campus or another—from Santiniketan and Delhi to Cambridge, Oxford, and Harvard—it was particularly thrilling for me to find that lecture halls and student accommodation can be such prominent findings in an excavation of ruins from more than a thousand years ago.

The old university at Nalanda was run by a Buddhist foundation, in what was then a very prosperous Bihar—the original centre of Buddhist religion, culture, and enlightenment—with its capital in Pataliputra (now called Patna) which also served, beginning in the third century BC, as the capital of the early empires of the Indian subcontinent for more than a thousand years. It is a matter of interest to note that Nalanda was the only institution of learning outside China to which any ancient Chinese ever went for higher education. As an institution of higher learning, where the entry qualifications were high, Nalanda was fed by a network of ancillary educational organizations. Some Chinese students, including the famous Yi Jing (635–713 AD), who studied in Nalanda for 10 years, and wrote the first inter-country comparative study of medical systems (comparing Chinese and Indian medical practices), first went to Sumatra (then the base of the Srivijaya empire) to learn Sanskrit, before coming to Nalanda. After acquiring his expertise in Sanskrit in the schools of Sumatra, Yi Jing took another boat journey, ending in Tamralipta (not far from modern-day Calcutta), on his way to Nalanda. There were four other Buddhism-related universities in Bihar by the seventh century, largely inspired by Nalanda, and they too played a collaborative role, though one of them—Vikramshila—emerged as a serious competitor to Nalanda for higher education by the tenth century.

After more than 700 years of successful pedagogy, old Nalanda was destroyed in the 1190s through a series of attacks by invading armies from West Asia, which also demolished the other universities in Bihar. There are serious debates on whether Bakhtiar Khilji, the ruthless invader whose conquering army ploughed through north India, was himself responsible for the sacking of Nalanda (as it is told in popular accounts), but the fact of the violent destruction by invading armies is quite well established. It is said that all the teachers and monks in Nalanda were killed, and the campus was razed to the

ground, special care being taken to demolish the beautiful statues spread across the campus of Buddha and other Buddhist
figures. The library, which was a tall building (it apparently had
nine stories), and was full of manuscripts, is reputed to have
burnt for three days. The destruction of Nalanda took place
shortly after the founding of Oxford University in 1167, and
about a decade before Cambridge University would be born in
1209. The patronage of higher learning by well-settled Muslim
kings (Mughals in particular) would come much later, by which
time nothing of Nalanda remained.

The Revival of Nalanda

The plan to re-establish the ancient institution of higher learning in Nalanda as a modern postgraduate university resulted
from a pan-Asian initiative. It germinated at home—in Patna and
Delhi—as well as abroad, particularly in Singapore. The formal
decision to revive old Nalanda was taken in 2007 by the East
Asia Summit (representing the ASEAN nations, combined with
a number of other eastern countries, including China, India,
Japan, Korea, Australia, and New Zealand), in their meeting in
Cebu in the Philippines. The re-establishment of Nalanda has
been led by a Mentor Group, which was later converted into the
Governing Board of the university. The group and the board are
firmly international in composition, and have members drawn
from a number of countries—from China and Japan to Singapore, Thailand, and the United Kingdom, in addition to India.

When Pranab Mukherjee (then Minister for External Affairs,
and now the President of India) called me at home to ask me

to chair the Nalanda Mentor Group, I felt, of course, much honoured, but also seriously challenged, given the obligations I already had related to research and teaching. I recognized that this would be a big responsibility to take on, and yet also realized that this was a unique opportunity to do something that I had always hoped would be done—indeed *must* be done. My discussion of the history of Nalanda in my book *The Argumentative Indian*, published in 2004, which had been translated into nearly every Asian language, generated much stronger interest, and elicited more frequent enquiries, as I travelled in Asia, than anything else in the book. It was not only hard for me to resist Pranab Mukherjee (a statesman I had reason to admire), but also difficult to abstain from the opportunity of replacing 'Perhaps one day', as an answer to speculations on the revival of Nalanda, with the proud affirmation: 'Right now—we are doing it'.

The revival of Nalanda University, led by the Mentor Group and then the Governing Board, has been taking place with help from India and abroad. The Government of India has been meeting the bulk of the financial needs—Manmohan Singh, as Prime Minister, expressed his strong support, and also promised full academic independence to Nalanda. To give Nalanda financial stability, the Singh government also made a commitment in early 2014 to meet Nalanda's regular expenses up to 2021.

Help has also come plentifully from the Government of Bihar, led by Chief Minister Nitish Kumar, with his own long-term vision of Nalanda (supported strongly by the then Deputy Chief Minister, Sushil Modi). The Government of Bihar has donated a large piece of land for re-establishing the old university, in Rajgir, about 15 kilometres from old Nalanda.

While help for rebuilding Nalanda has come from a number of Asian countries, the role of Singapore in this effort has been remarkably preeminent. It was in Singapore that a spectacular exhibition was held on the 'Nalanda Trail' in the Asian Civilizations Museum in 2007–8, giving a huge boost to the deliberations in the East Asia Summit on re-establishing the old university. It gathered together a wonderful collection of objects and historical accounts associated with the traditions and achievements of Buddhism in Asia, of which Nalanda was a critically important part, and arranged it all in an extraordinarily integrated way. Singapore has also established a research unit called the Nalanda-Sriwijaya Centre for work in related areas, linked with its Institute of Southeast Asian Studies.

George Yeo, the foreign minister of Singapore at that time, has been a major leader of the movement to re-establish Nalanda. He agreed to join the Mentor Group, and later the board, and I take this opportunity to note that our work would have been far harder—indeed almost impossibly difficult—but for George's wise counsel and insights. He also chairs the International Advisory Panel of Nalanda University, to which he has recruited some of the finest public figures in Asia. I also seize this occasion to note that enormous help has been provided to the conception and planning of the project by the insightful and hard-working board, with very distinguished members drawn from India and from the rest of Asia.[1] As its chair, I could not have been luckier.

A Progress Report

Restarting an old university after an 800-year hiatus is not an easy task. The work has, however, been robustly pursued by Vice-Chancellor Gopa Sabharwal and Dean Anjana Sharma. It is amazing to see how much has already been achieved through remarkable administrative leadership, including the establishment of curriculum, selection of teachers, choice of students, setting up of temporary premises for teaching, accommodation, and other services. There are still things to do, as the ongoing process of setting up new Nalanda proceeds full steam, but the difficult work of getting going is being done with splendid enthusiasm and efficiency.

The design and planning of the new campus is now completed for the early phases, after a thoroughgoing search for the right architectural firm (the famous Vastu Shilpa Consultants of India were chosen to work with us in this innovative job). The construction work is about to begin. However, since it will take a couple of years even for the early phase to be completed (leaving room for expansion later on), the new Nalanda has started functioning, in a small scale, from rented premises in Rajgir. Classes began, as promised, in September 2014, and the opening ceremony was graced by the presence of the Minister for External Affairs, Sushma Swaraj. It is her ministry that serves as the link between the Government of India and Nalanda University.

The international character of the educational engagement in Nalanda is already well established, despite the small initial intake of students and teachers. Students have come from near (from different parts of India and Bhutan) and far (including

Japan). The faculty already includes teachers not only from India, but also from abroad, including America, Germany, New Zealand, and Korea. Even though academic salaries in Nalanda are a lot lower than in America or Europe, there is much interest, judging from enquiries, among academics in different parts of the world, in joining, or at least trying out, the revived ancient university.

The choice of areas of teaching in the re-established Nalanda University is being governed both by budgetary considerations and by the relative importance of the respective fields, taking note of what is important in the tradition of Nalanda in relation to what is needed today, both locally and globally. The need for historical studies with a special focus on Asia is obvious enough, including the history of the so-called 'Nalanda Trail', and this does have contemporary relevance, both in terms of inspiration and the choice of research focus.

Along with the School of History, the new university has also started a School of Environmental Studies and Ecology. This is a neglected area of study not only in India, but also in Asia in general. There is also a strong need to supplement the rapidly growing understanding of global warming and other environmental hazards for the world as a whole, important as they are, by a greater comprehension and analysis of local environmental and ecological problems, including management problems of land, water, and forestry (even in the state of Bihar itself).

The vice-chancellor and the dean have worked hard to get international collaboration for the planning of teaching and research at Nalanda. For the development of environmental studies and ecology, Nalanda has been receiving collaborative help from Yale University's School of Forestry and also from the University of Illinois at Urbana-Champaign. For historical studies, there are ongoing collaborations with Chulalongkorn University in Thailand, the Institute of Southeast Asian Studies in Singapore, Peking University in Beijing, and the University of Minnesota.

The Governing Board has been engaged in considering what the next new schools should be. There is a popular demand, not least in Bihar itself, for a School of Economics, along with its connections with social development as well as management. A firm decision has been taken by the board to start a School of Economics from the academic year 2016-17. Another idea that is receiving consideration is the proposal, for which there is also a strong case, of having a School of Public Health. Not only is public health care in India in a state of much confusion right now, there is currently an astonishing neglect of education in public health in India. This is all the more striking because Yi Jing, the Nalanda student in the seventh century who was mentioned earlier, not only found much interest in public health in India, but in his comparison of Chinese and Indian medical practices, he also expressed his particular admiration for public health care in India (in contrast with pure medicine in which, Yi Jing thought, China had a clear edge over India). Yi Jing's praise of Indian public health care resonates also with the account of free public hospitals and medical services in India, particularly in Pataliputra, presented by another Chinese visitor, Faxian (Fa-Hien), in the early fifth century, shortly before Nalanda started functioning as an institution of higher learning.

Another school that is being considered is that of Buddhist Studies, Philosophy, and Comparative Religions. There is huge interest, both within India and abroad, to come to Nalanda for instruction and education on Buddhist ideas in general and their influence across Asia through what has been called the Nalanda Trail. The school planned would also provide the opportunity to study comparative religions in an academic—and philosophical—perspective.

While discussing accomplishments as well as hopes of further success, it is necessary to see whether any re-examination of old decisions may be needed. The fee for attending Nalanda University was originally fixed at Rs 300,000 per year, which amounts to Rs 600,000 for a two-year master's course. Although a 50 per cent subsidy was offered for the first batch of students, even Rs 300,000 over two years is still quite a high fee for most Indians (and students from the poorer Asian countries), and it is a strongly discouraging factor, particularly when many of the standard universities in India charge negligible fees. High fees, like those initially chosen for Nalanda, have, in fact, become quite common now in India for specialized education with business connections, for example, in the institutes of technology and of management, but the salary expectations of people receiving such technical education tend to be a great deal higher than what students receiving liberal education at Nalanda—or elsewhere—could expect to get. It is no shame for Nalanda that students completing their education in history, or in Buddhist studies, could not typically expect to have the kind of high salaries that trained managers and skilled engineers tend to get.

There are several different reasons for low student intake in the current—that is, the first—year in Nalanda. The newness of the institution and doubts about whether it would really start on time, as promised, deterred many potential applicants. The high entry qualifications embedded, rightly, in our criteria of admission also made it difficult for many applicants to be judged to be suitable. However, on top of that, the level of fees would have been a discouraging factor, and indeed a great many interested students told us that they would like to come to Nalanda if only they could afford it. The Governing Board had to consider different proposals on what the fees should rightly be (with different emphases on cost considerations and the opportunities of education offered by the university), but—after discussion—in the last meeting of the board last January, it was decided to cut the fees, to bring them in line with fees charged at the already established South Asia University. Accordingly, the board voted a big drop in the annual fees from Rs 300,000 to a level below Rs 60,000.

This change should make Nalanda a feasible choice for many more students. The fact remains, however, that even the new fees, though much lower, would remain too high for talented potential students from poorer background. There is, thus, a strong case for having generous provisions for student support on a selective basis. Further, since the big investments made to build up a campus and other facilities would not have adequate utilization in the absence of a fairly high student intake, and also since the initiative of reviving Nalanda will continue to have broader purposes, it is particularly important to seek support, including contributions to the endowment, which would allow the university to provide financial assistance to talented students from relatively poorer backgrounds to come to Nalanda to study.

The Government and Academic Independence

'Ritorno a Nalanda' was a remarkable moment, with the resumption of teaching in the world's oldest university, after a gap of many hundred years. But there has been further excitement in recent months—of a rather different kind—about governmental intervention in the running of Nalanda and the threats to its academic independence. Relations have been troubled between the newly elected Government of India and the Governing Board of Nalanda University (including myself as chancellor). The previous government (with the old Indian National Congress as the dominant partner of the UPA coalition), which initiated the revival of Nalanda University (in collaboration with the Government of Bihar and the East Asia Summit), comprehensively lost the general elections in the spring of 2014. The new Prime Minister, Narendra Modi of the Bharatiya Janata Party (BJP), who has long been an active member of the ideological fountainhead of the Hindutva movement, the Rashtriya Swayamsevak Sangh (RSS), is a more polarizing figure than were the previous BJP leaders, such as Atal Bihari Vajpayee. Given that, and also in view of the fact that I have freely spoken about my scepticism of Mr Modi's qualifications to lead a secular country, I was not entirely surprised to encounter governmental hostility to my continuing as chancellor of Nalanda University, coming from the Modi government, after their resounding electoral victory. If there was a personal element in the hostility (even though I have had good personal relations with many other BJP leaders), the bigger issue was that of the academic independence of Nalanda University, rather than its having to be in conformity with the political priorities of the ruling party.[2]

The unanimous recommendation of Nalanda's Governing Board, arrived at in my absence, in a meeting last January chaired by George Yeo of Singapore, that I should continue as chancellor, did not receive the endorsement of the visitor—the President of India—who has to act on the advice of the government. In fact, the Minister for External Affairs made it clear to board members who spoke with her that I was no longer acceptable as chancellor, and that the board must think of other names.

This may look like a matter of personal disapproval, which it must—at least partly—be. But there is, in fact, a bigger issue here of academic independence of institutions of higher learning that goes beyond personal issues. The new government has been active in trying to impose its own views on many academic institutions, and Nalanda is not the only such institution the intellectual independence of which has been under considerable threat in recent months. Nor is the removal of the chancellor the first occurrence of governmental interference in decisions of the Governing Board of Nalanda.[3] Many of the statutes dealing with the governance of Nalanda that were passed last year by the board (as it is authorized to do) have remained in abeyance, and have not even been presented to the visitor of the University—the President of India—for endorsement (as all such statutes formally require before they become effective). More actively, the government tried suddenly, without any consultation with—and without any communication to—the Governing Board, to reconstitute it radically. This move, however, did not work for legal reasons—in particular the fact that the proposed changes violated some provisions of the Nalanda University Act of the Indian Parliament.

The government's attempt to remove the chancellor has, however, been much more successful. The governmental non-acceptance of the decision of Nalanda's Governing Board led to a much-discussed tension between the board and the government. While I appreciated—and was moved by—the unanimous support I received from the board, it soon became clear to me that the conflict between the government and the Governing Board of Nalanda on the subject of my continuing as chancellor was proving to be a barrier to the urgent work of rebuilding Nalanda. It also became obvious to me that even if I were able to continue as chancellor (in line with the Governing Board's decision), governmental intervention would make me an ineffective leader for re-establishing Nalanda, and this surely could not be in the interest of the new university. So I decided to remove myself from being considered for re-appointment when my present term comes to an end in mid-July this year (while thanking the board warmly for their kind wish that I should continue).

In fact, I strongly believe that the personal identity of the chancellor is not of particular importance so long as a qualified person is appointed to the post, and the person understands the vision that lies behind Nalanda's revival and appreciates what Nalanda has to offer to contemporary higher education in India and elsewhere. It is, however, extremely important to make sure that in addition to the quality of leadership, the academic independence of Nalanda be respected, rather than its being buffeted by the politics of the day.

The conflict between Nalanda and the Indian government may seem to be about personalities, but actually it is about principles. It relates in particular to the importance of academic independence so that institutions of higher learning like Nalanda do not have to conform to the will and the whims of victorious politicians.

The interventions in Nalanda fit into a general pattern of interference by the present government in academic leadership across the country. For example, in January this year, when Sandip Trivedi, a renowned physicist, became the director of the Tata Institute of Fundamental Research (TIFR), perhaps the most prestigious scientific institution in India, chosen by a duly-constituted selection committee chaired by one of India's most well-known scientists, C.N.R. Rao, the Institute was told by the Prime Minister's Office that Trivedi must be removed from his post. Also in January, Raghunath Shevgaonkar, the well-known director of the Indian Institute of Technology Delhi, resigned from his position, alleging governmental interference in IIT's decisions. In March, Anil Kakodkar, one of India's leading nuclear scientists (and a former chair of the Indian Atomic Energy Commission) resigned from the chairmanship of the Governing Board of the Indian Institute of Technology Bombay, in protest against meddling by the government. Again, in late February, the government asked the writer A. Sethumadhavan to leave his position as chairman of the National Book Trust (which was set up decades ago as 'an autonomous body under the Ministry of Education'), so that this influential publishing position could be given to a

Hindutva ideologue, Baldev Sharma, former editor of the journal *Panchajanya*, which *The Times of India* describes as 'the RSS mouthpiece'.

The government has, I would argue, an inadequate appreciation of the distinction between (1) an autonomous institution supported by the government with the resources of the state, and (2) an institution under the command and dictate of the government currently in office. The universities in Europe, going back many hundreds of years, have been helped to become academically excellent through governmental respect for their autonomy. The British maintain academic independence in their own country with considerable care, even though the British rulers of colonial India very often violated the independence of public academic institutions. The Government of India seems to prefer the colonial model.

This is, of course, not the first time that a ruling Indian government has interfered in academic matters with its own views. The previous UPA government's record in non-interference was far from impeccable. But the extent of intervention has become extraordinarily common—and often politically extreme—under the present regime. And often enough, the persons chosen for heading institutions of national importance have been exceptionally dedicated to promoting Hindutva priorities. For example, the newly appointed head of the Indian Council of Historical Research (ICHR), Yellapragada Sudershan Rao, may not be known for research in history, but his Hindutva-oriented opinions are well-known. For example, in his paper 'Indian Caste System: A Reappraisal', Rao gives his endorsement to the caste system, which—we are told—is often "misrepresented as an exploitative system". Rao's strong links with Akhil Bharatiya

Itihas Sankalan Yojana (ABISY), which is known as the 'history wing' of the RSS, has been a matter of concern in the academic community, especially after four ABISY activists were appointed to the council of the ICHR. The chief editor of the official journal of ICHR (*Indian Historical Review*), the noted historian Sabyasachi Bhattacharya, resigned rather than having to work with the transformed ICHR.

Similarly, the new head of the Indian Council of Cultural Relations (ICCR), Lokesh Chandra, appointed by the Modi government, has informed *The Indian Express* that "from a practical point of view [Mr Modi] supersedes the Mahatma [Gandhi]". Chandra has also shared with us his view that Modi is, in fact, "a reincarnation of God". Commenting on Korean civilization, the head of the Indian Council revealed his belief that six million Koreans trace their ancestry back to an Indian princess from Ayodhya.

Given all this, Nalanda University has reason to be cautiously hopeful that there is a possible compromise that seems to be emerging— with the strong likelihood, at the time of writing this essay, of having an East Asian chancellor, in particular George Yeo, who has been a major architect in the re-establishing of Nalanda. This is not, however, accidental good fortune, and the public's interest in the subject, it would appear, has had an important role in making this possible. The subject of the government's interference in Nalanda's governance got politicized early (since the issue of the chancellor's removal was much discussed in the media), and it drew considerable critical public attention. The debates surrounding the confrontation between the government and the Governing Board received a lot of media coverage and extensive public scrutiny, and these developments have certainly helped to have a restraining effect on the government, unlike in the case of many other academic institutions. It has also helped the Minister for External Affairs, Sushma Swaraj in her resolve to have a solution that would be publicly defendable—rather than follow the unilateral extremism characterizing many of the academic interventions by the Modi government.

The presence of many intellectuals from other Asian countries in the Governing Board of Nalanda has also contributed to the avoidance of a sectarian imposition. The board, which I continue to chair (until mid-July), has proposed in a meeting in early May that one of the non-Indian Asian members of the board be appointed chancellor, placing the name of George Yeo of Singapore at the top of the list, with two other distinguished Asians (Wang Bangwei of China and Susumu Nakanishi of Japan) as reserves. Yeo has been persuaded to accept this position, subject to the government giving him the independence that the running of Nalanda demands, and at the time of writing this essay, it seems quite likely that he will indeed be the next chancellor of Nalanda University. Given Yeo's commitment to the exacting vision of Nalanda, in addition to his remarkable intellectual and administrative skills, this would indeed be a good solution.

So there is a possibility of a happy ending there. However, it will remain extremely important for the government to live up to our hope that Yeo will have the independence he would need to make Nalanda an academic success in line with its vision, rather than its going down the sectarian way the ICHR and the ICCR have gone.

Why Revive Nalanda?

There is reason for satisfaction that new Nalanda has started functioning as promised, on time, though, for the moment, on a rather small scale. A successful beginning does not, however, eliminate the need for critical scrutiny of the entire project of reviving Nalanda University. What is the relevance of Nalanda in the contemporary world? When the old Nalanda began functioning as a university, there was no other university in the world, and its need was obvious. In contrast, new Nalanda is joining a very large group of institutions of higher learning in the world. In India alone there are 687 universities already—and others may be coming up even as I write. So why one more?

It is true that the revived Nalanda University will not be just a new university, but quite special, even unique. But we must ask what will be so special about it, other than its claim to an old historical link? We understand the glory of old Nalanda, but why not rest with celebrating what was a huge past achievement, rather than, to put it provocatively, cluttering up our present with debris from a long lost past? Should we not look to the future rather than to the past? These are indeed legitimate and reasonable doubts.

One of the areas in which Indian universities have been less than distinguished, with a few notable exceptions, is the pursuit of original research. Even when the quality of teaching has been good (which, alas, is often not the case), research performance has tended to be relatively limited in the Indian universities, including in those with highly successful record in pedagogy, such as the IITs. Research orientation is one of the priorities that India's former president, Abdul Kalam, who has been a leading supporter of the idea of reviving Nalanda, has particularly urged on the new university. A definitive record of research achievement will undoubtedly take time to accomplish, but the demands of that priority have to be firmly borne in mind in creating and safeguarding research opportunities in the new university. In this context, the inspirational quality of old Nalanda is a great help. What brought thousands of students from across Asia to Nalanda is the understanding that new ideas and epistemic departures animated that famous institution. Judging by the interests and backgrounds of those seeking faculty positions in Nalanda (and also of those wanting to study in Nalanda), something of that dazzling historical memory still motivates those wanting to join Nalanda. With suitable opportunities, a dream can indeed become a reality.

There is also something in the basic understanding behind old Nalanda that still remains substantively important today. The tradition of Nalanda was not only that of quality education—itself a matter of great importance in India today with its remarkable lack of quality control in education at all levels—but also the pursuit of global cooperation, including a systematic attempt to learn across the barriers of regions and countries. What the Asian Civilizations Museum in Singapore called the Nalanda Trail is based on a flow of ideas and contacts that brought people together from different countries and different historical backgrounds. The need for that one-world perspective has become even stronger over the centuries.

It is easy to see how profoundly the commitment reflected in the Nalanda Trail was inspired by Gautama Buddha's focus on enlightenment without borders, for all people. This issue came up, in fact, in a conversation in the seventh century when one of Nalanda's most distinguished Chinese students, Xuan Zang (602–664 AD), completed his studies and was considering going back to China. The professors at Nalanda offered Xuan Zang (also known as Hiuen Tsang) a faculty position, asking him to stay on in Nalanda as a professor. Xuan Zang turned the offer down on the ground, among others, that Buddha had taught the world not to enjoy enlightenment alone. If one learns something, it is one's duty to share it with others, and therefore he must go home and do just that. Indeed, the vast sweep of Buddhist enlightenment across China, Japan, Korea, Thailand, and much of East Asia was so successful because, I would argue, it largely came not just as an imposition of foreign ideas (which to some extent it must have been), but mainly as a sharing of enlightenment and a new understanding of what binds people together.[4] There is a grandness of vision there that needs focus and emphasis today in our very divisive world. Indeed, recently some Buddhist organizations have themselves been used for fomenting divisions—and for generating violent confrontations—for example, against Rohingya Muslims in Rakhine in Burma. This is a huge departure not only from the integrative tradition of Nalanda, but also from Buddha's own teachings in general (not to mention the Buddhist principles on peace and tolerance canonized on stone tablets by Emperor Ashoka across India—and abroad). Nalanda's education was broad and liberal, and it drew its support from non-Buddhist communities as well (for example, the Hindu emperors of India, such as the Guptas, were among the patrons of Nalanda). It offered education on secular subjects as well as on non-Buddhist religious texts. And as Xuan Zang recorded, education in Nalanda was not only offered through the 'bestowing' of knowledge by lecturers, but through long debates on different subjects. Indeed, it was widely noted that Nalanda established a genre of education through discussion that was both innovative and powerfully effective.

The need for a critically engaged but non-confrontational global perspective, in the way Buddha emphasized, is not any less today than it has been in the past.[5] As we open our morning papers now, we see daily reports of violence coming from across the world that draw on different groups' divisive—and sometimes confrontational—commitments, linked in one way or another with their respective readings of the past. To say that we should look only to the future, not the past, overlooks the fact that the past is in our present. Indeed, much of the world today is as flammable and violent as it is precisely because readings of the past are often used to feed confrontation rather than cooperation in our present-day world. If the revived Nalanda University succeeds in becoming a distinguished university in the modern world, as I very much hope it will, and continues to focus on broad-minded study of history and culture, it will be in a position to contribute significantly to global understanding across the boundaries of nations, communities, and religions.

As was mentioned earlier, one of the two schools—or faculties—with which new Nalanda has begun is that of history, and the curriculum has a special focus on the history of cross-border interactions and cooperation, particularly in Asia. It would, however, be important to clarify here that the commitment of historical studies in Nalanda is to veracity and truthful understanding, not to promoting any particular ethics, *even one of harmony*. If the old Nalanda contributed to the spread of ideas and enlightenment across borders, it was not because it obliterated divisive readings of the past as being inadmissible. Critical search for a sustainable understanding is also what new Nalanda's commitment is, and there will be no departure from the exacting demands of epistemology. If there is an ethical commitment to peace and mutual help, that commitment does not have to be promoted by overlooking the various factors and causal forces that cause the opposite of peace and cooperation. Practical reason, to use that old fashioned word, can draw both from epistemic rigour and from clear-headed moral and political arguments. One of the reasons why students like Xuan Zang were so full of admiration for their famous teacher Shilabhadra—about whom Xuan Zang kept on enquiring even after he had returned to China—is because he (Shilabhadra) could advance sustainable ethical reasoning without having to take any kind of leave from the demands of epistemology. There is certainly a huge vision there from which modern Nalanda can powerfully benefit.

What kind of new understanding can we expect from the re-engagement with history, without losing the demands of veracity? Let me give an example, drawn from a debate in which I was privileged to participate with the teachers and students of new Nalanda last October. One of the dominant influences in understanding the contact and intercourse between Asia and Europe is the impact and influence of what is called the Silk Route. Extending over 4,000 miles, this was the route through which merchandise moved between Asia and Europe. Silk was one of the principal exports of China—hence the name. Originally established between the third century BC and the third century AD, during the Han Dynasty, the Silk Route was of profound importance not only for trade and commerce, but also for the intermingling of people and ideas.

The critical question that can be asked is not about the importance of the Silk Route, nor about the crucial role of trade in linking people with each other across borders. Neither is in dispute. It is, rather, about whether an exaggerated focus on trade and commodity exchange in human contacts, and related to that a magnified reading of the role of the Silk Route, may contribute to the downplaying of other influences through which people interact with each other across frontiers and borders, including the massive civilizational interactions that the Nalanda Trail generated and sustained.

In fact, there have been some attempts recently even to see old Nalanda itself as a by-product of the Silk Route. That, I would argue, would be a huge mistake. This is not merely because Nalanda was not on—or even strongly linked with—the Silk Route, but also because Nalanda was central to a different avenue of interaction in which trade of commodities was not the prime mover. If trade gets people together (and it certainly does), then so does interest in knowledge and enlightenment. Mathematics, science, engineering, and the arts, along with religious and ethical commitments, have moved people across regions, by land and across the seas, in pursuit of human interest in them. The important point is that the motivation behind these journeys was not the pursuit of commercial gain, but search for ideas. The huge popularity of seeing global connections only through the prism of trade, of which the Silk Route is a leading example, should not be allowed to eclipse the fact that reflective engagements have also moved people across countries and regions over millennia. The Silk Route is rightly celebrated in world history (a part of it—the Chang' an-Tianshan Corridor—is also recognized by the UNESCO as a World Heritage Centre), in a way that the gigantic influence of the Nalanda Trail has not yet been adequately grasped (in fact Nalanda has not yet received any kind of recognition by the United Nations as a World Heritage Centre).

Given the importance of reflective interconnections in the world, this is both an issue of past history and one of a contemporary vision of an intellectually engaged world. Old Nalanda belonged solidly to a globally interactive tradition, the need for which remains strong today. The campus of new Nalanda that is being built a few miles away from old Nalanda is at the edge of the old town of Rajgir. In fact, it is in Rajgir—then called Rajagriha—that Gautama Buddha had talked with some of his early followers. And it was in that ancient town that the first Buddhist Council had met, shortly after Buddha's death, to discuss how to resolve differences through debates and arguments, rather than remaining stuck in unresolved disagreements.

For me personally, Rajgir is a very familiar place, since in my school days I used to go regularly to Rajgir with other students at Santiniketan, along with a couple of our teachers, to camp at the foot of the majestic Rajgir hills and trace the old Buddhist trails (I also remember with amusement how some early romances developed and foundered among the students of co-educational Santiniketan, without seriously interfering with our pursuit of Buddhist trails). When I visited Rajgir again more than half a century later in the context of re-establishing Nalanda, I found it to be almost unrecognizably changed by the invasion of chaotic urbanity. And yet, of course, it had the same Buddhist trails and evoked the same historical recollection of the Buddhist Council in the sixth century BC—with its pioneering commitment to resolve differences through discussion and dialogue.

It is a later Buddhist Council—the third—which met in Pataliputra at the invitation of Emperor Ashoka in the third century BC, that is most famous, both because of its largeness and because of the importance of the difficult issues that were resolved there through discussion. And yet Nalanda sits right next to the location of the very first attempt, possibly in the world, of what in the nineteenth century Walter Bagehot would call, following John Stuart Mill, "government by discussion". Old Nalanda, which came up next to ancient Rajgir, belonged to that tradition, and even used debates as a principal means of education (as Xuan Zang and others had noted). There is a history there that is both inspirational and instructive, focusing on a priority that remains relevant and useful in the contemporary world. 'Ritorno a Nalanda' can be more than a moment of local jubilation.

Notes and References

1. The board members are Mr George Yeo (Singapore), Professor Wang Bangwei (China), Professor Susumu Nakanishi (Japan), Professor Wang Gungwu (Singapore), Professor Assavavirulhakarn Prapod (Thailand), Professor Lord [Meghnad] Desai (UK/India), Professor Sugata Bose (India), Mr N.K. Singh (India), Professor Tansen Sen (India), Mr Anil Wadhwa (Secretary East), and Dr Gopa Sabharwal (Vice-Chancellor). In the critically important period, we were assisted by the Nalanda Monitoring Committee, led by Mr Montek Singh Ahluwalia, then the deputy chair of India's Planning Commission.

2. I have discussed this episode more fully in an essay forthcoming in *The New York Review of Books*.

3. The interferences have sometimes been accompanied by the planting of false reports, typically through statements to the media. Some examples of the crudeness of the attack can be seen in the much publicized public statement of a prominent BJP leader that the Nalanda chancellor is "paid an annual salary of Rs 50 lakh" (rather than no salary at all), or that "so far about Rs 3000 crore" have been spent by Nalanda University (in fact, rather less than 2 per cent of that sum—around Rs 46 crore—has been expended altogether, including construction costs, from the very beginning of the university up to the end of the last financial year, 2014–15). On misinformation put out to the media by the government itself, see the news interview with Professor Sugata Bose, a member of the Nalanda Governing Board (and also a Member of the Indian Parliament), published in *The Telegraph*, Kolkata, 1 April 2015.

4. On this subject, see also William Dalrymple, 'The Great and Beautiful Lost Kingdoms', *New York Review of Books*, 21 May 2015.

5. On this subject, see my essay 'The Contemporary Relevance of Buddha', *Ethics and International Affairs*, volume 28, number 1 (Carnegie Council for Ethics in International Affairs, 2014), pp. 15–27.

NAME INDEX

SUBJECT INDEX

ABOUT THE AUTHOR

One of the world's foremost thinkers, Amartya Sen studied in Patha Bhavan (Santiniketan), Presidency College (Calcutta), and Trinity College (Cambridge, UK). He is Thomas W. Lamont University Professor and Professor of Economics and Philosophy at Harvard University. He is also Senior Fellow at the Harvard Society of Fellows. Earlier, he was Professor of Economics at Jadavpur University, Calcutta, the Delhi School of Economics, and the London School of Economics; Drummond Professor of Political Economy at Oxford University; and Master of Trinity College, Cambridge University.

Sen has served as President of the Econometric Society, the American Economic Association, the Indian Economic Association, and the International Economic Association. His research has ranged over social choice theory, economic theory, ethics and political philosophy, welfare economics, theory of measurement, decision theory, development economics, public health, and gender studies. His books have been translated into more than 30 languages, and include *Choice of Techniques* (1960), *Growth Economics* (1970), *Collective Choice and Social*

Welfare (1970), *Choice, Welfare and Measurement* (1982), *Commodities and Capabilities* (1987), *The Standard of Living* (1987), *Development as Freedom* (1999), *Identity and Violence: The Illusion of Destiny* (2006), *The Idea of Justice* (2009), and, with Jean Drèze, *An Uncertain Glory: India and Its Contradictions* (2013).

Sen's awards include the Bharat Ratna (India), Commandeur de la légion d'honneur (France), the National Humanities Medal (USA), Ordem Nacional do Mérito Científico (Brazil), Honorary Companion of Honour (UK), Aztec Eagle (Mexico), Edinburgh Medal (UK), the George Marshall Award (USA), the Eisenhower Medal (USA), and the Nobel Prize in Economics.

I wish a day for a week